Understanding Adult Survivors
of Domestic Violence in Childhood

Still Forgotten, Still Hurting

Understanding Adult Survivors of Domestic Violence in Childhood

Still Forgotten, Still Hurting

GILL HAGUE WITH ANN HARVEY AND KATHY WILLIS

Jessica Kingsley *Publishers*
London and Philadelphia

First published in 2012
by Jessica Kingsley Publishers
116 Pentonville Road
London N1 9JB, UK
and
400 Market Street, Suite 400
Philadelphia, PA 19106, USA

www.jkp.com

Library of Congress Cataloging in Publication Data
Hague, Gill.
  Understanding adult survivors of domestic violence in childhood : still
forgotten, still hurting / Gill Hague, with Ann Harvey and Kathy Willis.
    p. cm.
  Includes bibliographical references and index.
  ISBN 978-1-84905-096-8 (alk. paper)
  1. Family violence--Psychological aspects. 2. Victims of family
violence. 3. Children and violence--Psychological aspects. 4. Psychic
trauma in children. I. Harvey, Ann. II. Willis, Kathy. III. Title.
  HV6626.H254 2012
  362.82'924--dc23
                            2012019080

British Library Cataloguing in Publication Data
A CIP catalogue record for this book is available from the British Library

ISBN 978 1 84905 096 8
eISBN 978 0 85700 279 2

Printed and bound in Great Britain

To all those adults who experienced domestic violence as children.

On behalf of Gill Hague:
As this is my last book, to all the violence against women activists, survivors and practitioners with whom I have worked over 40 years. To Dorothy, Elizabeth and Tom in memoriam, and to Cassie, Dave and Keiran, with great love.

On behalf of Ann Harvey:
To Chris and Andy with deepest love and thanks for your company on my journey into feminism and the search for greater possibilities in our relationships as women and men. To all the children and young people with whom I have worked: there are no adequate words to express my appreciation and thanks for being allowed to share your journeys to recovery, for your courage and for all that you have taught me. May your futures be safe and full of love and play.

Contents

List of poems

Acknowledgements

This book would not have been possible without the insights and help of many people. First, our thanks to all the survivors of domestic abuse with whom we have interacted over the years and who, through their courage, expertise and resilience, have given us so much. Second, we would like to thank all the practitioners, policy-makers, violence against women workers and activists who have shared their knowledge and insights with us.

Particular thanks to the adults who had experienced domestic violence as children who were specifically interviewed in depth, and to the members of the lengthy focus group, whose insights and advice form part of the backbone of the book. All the participants gave us their time and knowledge willingly and sometimes at some emotional cost, while also agreeing that, in the end, the focus group and interviews had been personally empowering. All were deeply committed to contributing to the book in order to assist others facing the same life traumas that they had faced.

Our sincere gratitude, in particular, to the poets and testimony-givers. The various poets who contributed to this book were all women. Often working closely with the first author, they expressed their own personal experiences in a series of beautiful, brave and painful poems.

The three testimony-givers contributed personal stories that are moving and beautifully presented. Writing these painful testimonies was a labour of love and commitment for all of them. They all drew profoundly on their own emotional resilience in order to reflect so honestly on their experiences as children, to revisit the past and to construct powerful pieces of writing. They also offer advice to other adults with such childhood experiences. It is an honour to have their testimonies in this book which bring it vividly to life, together with the unique and powerful poems.

Our special gratitude to Vicki Banyard from the University of New Hampshire, who was an International Visiting Fellow at the Centre for Gender and Violence Research in Bristol in 2010, and who met with the first author on several occasions about the book, contributed her own related and authoritative work extensively, and gave sensitive and invaluable advice on various chapters.

Thanks also, and as ever, to Nicola Harwin, the Chief Executive of the national UK domestic violence charity, Women's Aid and to Ellen Malos,

Centre for Gender and Violence Research, University of Bristol and Co-founder of the original Domestic Violence Research Group. They have enriched both our lives (particularly the first author's) and the struggle against violence against women beyond measure. Nicola also commented helpfully on the text.

Cathy Humphreys and Lucy Healey from the University of Melbourne spent much time locating and sending relevant articles, way beyond the call of duty. Very many thanks to them. The texts enriched the book. Marianne Hester also provided references, key books and (as always) authoritative insights on the subject of children and domestic violence for which we are most grateful.

People who offered particular help, materials or insights (sometimes responding to requests for assistance and sometimes without realising it) are too numerous to mention but include, in alphabetical order, Ann Devereaux, Geetanjali Gangoli, Aisha Gill, MaryAnn Hushlak, Liz Kelly, Lucy (surname withheld), the late Joseph M. (surname withheld), Audrey Mullender, Lorraine Radford, Ravi Thiara and Pam Trevithick. Thanks also to all the members of the Centre for Gender and Violence Research.

Cassie Hague, Lynn-Marie Sardinha and, most especially, Debbie Allnock contributed very helpfully and at some length on the manuscript drafts. Dave Merrick contributed ideas, ongoing in-depth discussion of the issues, advice on content and structure, emotional support and detailed edits. Our sincere thanks to him.

Our gratitude to Jessica Kingsley Publishers for very helpful publishing, editing and correcting assistance.

A special mention, for Gill, of Joe (Urch), Barista par excellence at Acapellas's cafe who served her endless super-hot, flat lattes while she wrote on her laptop – always with a smile, pleasantries to share – and 'Your usual, Gill?'

Last of all, particular thanks to our dear friends, mentors, partners and family members for emotional support and caring.

For Ann: Chris Harvey, Andrew Harvey, Jeannie Osmond, Jeannette Chipping, Bridget Walker and Alexander Esterhuyzen. For Kathy: Amber Williams, Sue Willis (Kathy's mum), Jason Willis, Luke Willis, Tom Willis, Gill Hague and Anna Bianchi. For Gill: Cassie Hague, Keiran Merrick, Dave Merrick, Alison Assiter and the late Dorothy Williamson. You have all given us more than you can ever know. Thank you.

Chapter 1

Adults who were Exposed to Domestic Violence as Children

Introduction and Background

ARMS OUTSTRETCHED TO THEM

[1]
She couldn't help remembering,
even though she's well past 50.
Arms outstretched to them.
The pain comes sharp at the back of her mouth.

She couldn't help remembering.
It won't go away.

Hurrying anxiously back from school,
knowing she had to go back into that hurtful house,
where she loved everyone so much.
The feeling of the shades coming down.

She couldn't help remembering,
her glowing mother.

Just a young woman really,
making her dresses,
cooking home-made cakes,
laughing with the children in the garden,
loving them with a deep brave fierceness.

And the light gradually going out of her eyes.

Turning bitter and argumentative,
being awkward
or martyred.

Her father crushed with disappointment too.

[II]
She couldn't help remembering,
even though she's well past 50.

The feeling of the shades coming down.

Her father mad with fury.

But she couldn't stop it,
couldn't stop him.
Crying and sobbing,
tears dripping off her chin.
She couldn't stop him.

She couldn't help remembering.

And she learned not to sleep.
She dreaded anyone suspecting.

She couldn't help remembering.

Her expectant young life reduced to
what felt like fragments,

bitter
and a tangled feeling.

She couldn't help remembering.

Even though she's well past 50,

But she couldn't stop it,
crying and sobbing,
arms outstretched to them.

Even though she's well past 50.

She couldn't stop it. Even though she's well past 50. If you've experienced domestic violence as a child, you might feel similarly to 'Juliette', the 55-year-old Scottish woman who contributed this and other poems to the book. It doesn't go away. You can't stop it. It is always there, ready to jump back at you, sometimes when you least expect it. When you think you've got over it. Even when you're well past 50, or 30, or 70.

This book is the first of its type, and it is dedicated to adult survivors of domestic violence experiences, which happened when they were children. It is about people whose parents or carers perpetrated or experienced domestic abuse, and whose childhood was damaged by the experience, sometimes leaving them with scars into and throughout adulthood.

As a 'first of its type', it has a slightly different form to a standard book about domestic abuse. Rather than being a book solely for professionals, researchers, activists, or students, written as an academic or practitioner text, the content is instead a mixture of academic and creative writing. Poetry and testimony have been included to enhance the content. The idea is that the creative and directly personal material illustrates, grounds and 'makes real' the more academic and practice-oriented sections.

Thus, the book is founded in real experience and creative expression to humanise it and to enrich the experience of reading or studying it, without compromising academic robustness. Feminists have, since the 1970s, suggested that: 'the personal is political'. Here, the aim is not only to present discussions of the reality of childhood domestic violence for adults and to provide material on professional, practical and academic responses to it, but also to use the personal and the creative to shed an enlightening lens on these discussions.

For the first author, this is the last book of my own career during which I have worked for about 40 years on the subject of violence against women and domestic abuse, as an activist, practitioner, social worker, academic and researcher. In latter years, I have worked as Professor of Violence Against Women Studies, one of only a few to have this type of appellation across the world, which honours the addressing of gendered violence within the social sciences. This book represents a personal ending of both emotional and professional resonance.[1]

The reasons for writing and coordinating it are complex. Conducting collaborative research on children's experiences of domestic violence in the late 1990s and early 2000s (see Hague, Malos and Dear 1996; Humphreys *et al.* 2000; Mullender *et al.* 2002) and following up adult survivors of violence whom I had known over many years, it became clear to me that there was a gap in the field. The subject of adult survivors of childhood domestic abuse tends to be dealt with either in regard to adults experiencing domestic abuse themselves as adults, or in regard to the children of victims and perpetrators. Attention has rarely been focused, with the exception perhaps of individual therapy and counselling sessions, on adults who grew up in households which were domestically violent or who otherwise experienced violence between the adults in their lives, and who have lived with the experience into maturity. This book attempts to fill the gap.

---

1   During these many years of work on gender violence, I have also produced over 100 publications, so this last book, with its unusual structure, is an emotive final journey.

To be clear: what do we mean by domestic violence?

In this book, the terms 'domestic violence' and 'domestic abuse' are used more or less interchangeably. Women's Aid, the UK domestic violence charity, is the main provider of both domestic violence and sexual violence services in the country. The Women's Aid definition of domestic abuse is used in the book, and is:

> Physical, sexual, psychological or financial violence that takes place within an intimate or family-type relationship and forms a pattern of coercive and controlling behaviour. This can include forced marriage and so-called 'honour' crimes. Domestic violence may include a range of abusive behaviours, not all of which are in themselves inherently 'violent'. (Women's Aid 2010)

Thus, so-called 'honour'-based violence and forced marriage (as opposed to arranged marriage in which the parties consent) are currently regarded as issues of domestic violence (see Gangoli, Razak and McCarry 2006; Gill 2006), and many definitions now contain a reference to coercive control, sometimes continual and long-term, by the abuser over the abused (see Stark 2007).

Domestic violence can occur in a range of relationships including those which are heterosexual, gay, lesbian, bisexual or transgendered, and also within extended families (Women's Aid 2010). Most researchers and policy-makers, as well as specialist agencies, agree that the vast majority of intimate violence is experienced by women. Perpetrators are most commonly male, although abuse can also occur the other way round against men (see Gadd et al. 2002; Hester 2009). Thus, while individuals requesting assistance from helping agencies will overwhelmingly be women, this is not to belittle the need of male victims for appropriate help, counselling, advocacy and support. This book will, it is to be hoped, be of help to all adult victims of childhood domestic violence, both men and women. However, it is mainly framed in terms of domestic violence against women, the huge majority of victims across the world.

There is some agreement among organisations addressing gendered violence nationally and internationally, including Women's Aid in the UK, that intimate violence may be experienced regardless of ethnicity, religion, class, caste, age, sexuality, disability or lifestyle, although it may take a variety of cultural forms. (It should be noted, however, that domestic violence against disabled women is rarely adequately dealt with in definitions: see, for example, Hague *et al.* 2008). In general, this type of violence includes sexual assault and rape within intimate relationships as well as physical, financial and emotional abuse, and is distressingly widespread.

A pioneering international study of domestic violence across many countries, the *Multi-country Study of Health and Domestic Violence Against Women*, was conducted by the World Health Organisation and completed in 2005 (WHO 2005). The study was based on interviews with 24,000 women over 15 sites and 11 countries, namely: Bangladesh, Brazil, Ethiopia, Japan, Namibia, Peru, Samoa, Serbia and Montenegro, Thailand and the United Republic of Tanzania. The research was also replicated by New Zealand, with closely related surveys in Chile, China, Indonesia and Vietnam, and concluded that violence against women is both extremely widespread and demands a public health response across the world (WHO 2005).

The studies showed very high levels of physical domestic violence globally, being experienced by from 29 to 62 per cent of women, with the comparable figures for sexual violence being 30 per cent and 56 per cent. Most studies in the UK find that around one in four women experience physical domestic violence across a lifetime, with one in eight to one in ten experiencing intimate abuse of this type at any one time (Hague and Malos 2005; Women's Aid 2010). Overall, the World Health Organisation informs us (WHO 2005) that between one in five and one in three women worldwide experience physical violence from their intimate partners – from the person with whom they share perhaps their closest, most tender moments and who may profess to love them. It is worth reiterating this extremely high percentage – up to one in three of the world's women experience some form of intimate violence, as estimated by the most prestigious health organisation in the world.

How the book is structured

This book is specifically concerned with the ongoing impact of domestic violence on children when they have grown up to be adults. In more detail, it looks at what we know and what we may feel about the issue of adult survivors of childhood domestic abuse, as well as at what we can do about it. It combines discussions of academic research to provide information and research evidence on which we can draw, with ideas for good practice for practitioners and professionals in the field. The good practice guidance is presented both in terms of working with adults, and in terms of working with children to try to address the issues before the person concerned grows up.

Practical and therapeutic suggestions for those actually in the situation are interspersed with personal testimonies by adults who experienced domestic abuse as children and with poems, also by survivors. As the main author, I am most grateful to the contributors of the three personal testimonies, all of which are anonymised. Two of these are by women, one young woman and one in her mid-years, and one is by a man in his sixties. The poems are also all anonymised, or the names used are not the author's real name. Some of the poetry has been directly commissioned for the book and the poets concerned have produced moving, painful and beautiful poems especially for this project. Some have been written jointly with the first author, but the content in each case is the individual poet's own. All of those who have contributed to the book have spoken of their enduring hurt at the experiences they had as children. Producing the poems and testimonies in many cases has been distressing, although ultimately cathartic, and, for some, it has been the first time the authors have spoken out about their experiences. Heartfelt thanks to them all.

One of the co-authors is Ann Harvey who was, until recently, an NSPCC (National Society for the Prevention of Cruelty to Children) Children's Services Practitioner (social worker) providing a post-abuse therapeutic recovery service for children, many of whom had experienced domestic abuse. She is also a campaigner against domestic violence. Ann joined the writing team to contribute lengthy sections to our joint chapter on direct work with children who have experienced domestic abuse. The idea in this chapter is that good practice with children can enable recovery and happier childhoods now, and prevent later distress and trauma for adults in the future. It should be noted that Ann writes in a personal capacity and the views expressed in this book are not necessarily those of the NSPCC. The second co-author of this book is Kathy Willis who works, in both a professional and a volunteer capacity, to offer emotional support and advocacy to women who have experienced sexual and domestic violence. Both Ann and Kathy monitored and commented on the overall content, and wrote material for inclusion in various sections.

There is not a great deal of academic literature about adults who have experienced childhood domestic abuse (although there is more material from North America). Most of the literature of this type is on children and is discussed more fully in Chapter 2, to give a foundation for the later discussions about adults. Chapter 3 looks at the actual research that has been conducted on the impact, in adulthood, of witnessing domestic abuse as children. Chapter 4 discusses the painful impacts that this type of childhood violence can have in adult life, drawing principally on what adult survivors themselves say. Information is presented from the outcomes of a focus group with six adults who had had childhood experiences of abuse and 15 further interviews. Chapter 6 looks at how to work in practical and therapeutic ways with children to try to prevent damaging outcomes in the future for the adults they later become. Leading on from this consideration, Chapter 8 discusses, in detail, how to work with adults themselves in this situation, and suggests practical and healing ways forward. As a key chapter for those using this book in order to recover emotionally and practically, it is designed both for adult survivors of such personal childhood experiences and for practitioners, agencies, counsellors and policy-makers, to offer guidance and recommendations for good practice. The personal testimonies and poetic material are interspersed between these chapters, with the testimonies themselves in Chapters 5, 7 and 9. Chapter 10 is the conclusion, suggesting that recovery, and an end to the anguish of childhood domestic abuse, is possible.

This is a painful subject and people reading the book who have had childhood experiences of domestic violence may find it brings up unpleasant or upsetting memories, in which case getting some support and sympathetic help is to be recommended. The practice ideas in Chapter 8 may be of some help in achieving this, both for individual survivors and for counsellors, therapists, domestic violence workers and social workers. The idea of the book for those with direct life experience of the issue is that it might offer a kind of healing experience and some ways forward to transform grief, loss and hurt into human enrichment and fulfilment. This chapter finishes with 'Kate's' painful experiences in her powerful and sad poem, commissioned for this book, not using her real name and written in collaboration with the main author. For 'Kate', the past won't go away.

FOR KATE, THE PAST WON'T GO AWAY

[1]
The tears come easy to Kate.

The churning stomach.
The feeling of having no right in this world,
no right to be seen or respected or regarded
as worth much at all.

No.
The tears come easy to Kate.
She knows she's in the wrong.

You're too fragile, they tell her,
too easily knocked off course,
too easily hurt.

You need to get some backbone, Kate.

The tears leap up, when she should be strong.
Yes,
she should be.

Yes.
She knows they are right.
She should get that backbone.
See, she's wrong again.

On the backbone front this time.

[II]
She knows she is hopeless, fragile, no good…

But I *am* fragile
and that doesn't have to be bad,
thinks Kate at her best.

I *was* fragile when I was little.
That was the result of it all.

And fragile is also precious,
she reflects achingly sometimes.

Fragile is also human and to be treasured.

Fragile is also beautiful.

Think of fine silk or a precious turquoise feather,
she wants to say,

fighting tears again,

but she doesn't.

[III]
Kate often feels
it's not fair to put the blame on the violence
when she was a child.

It's not fair to blame her father.

Of course not.

See, she's wrong yet again.

She needs to be responsible for it all herself.
Yes.
And for the empty gaps.

But she can't do it.
It's too fractured and messy.

It's not fair to say it's his fault or their fault, is it?
No.

But
then her friends contradict her.
Yes.

It is fair and only right, they tell her.

See. Yet again she feels wrong-footed and guilty.

The tears come easy to Kate,

The churning stomach.
The feeling of having no right in this world.

[IV]
The tears come easy.
She feels fragile again.

But fragile is also precious,
Kate still thinks

in the good moments.

Fragile is also human and to be treasured,

she wants to say again,
But her confidence doesn't last.

She can't say it.

She hates herself
for not being able to say it.

Even though she believes it.

And feels fragilely beautiful at her best.
Yes.

Well,
No.
The tears come easy to Kate.

Kate's poem continues in Chapter 4.

Chapter 2

Before You Grow Up

What the Research Tells Us about Children who Experience Domestic Violence

In order to prepare the ground for looking at the experiences of adults who have experienced domestic abuse in childhood and who still carry the impacts, we first consider those impacts on children themselves before they grow up. Readers wishing to concentrate on adults who lived with, or witnessed, childhood domestic violence, and on ways to deal with this life situation, may choose to skip both this chapter and Chapter 6 which are specifically about children. However, if domestic abuse in children's lives can be prevented, or if therapeutic and advocacy interventions can assist them to recover, then the outcome for the adults they later become will be enhanced.

Thus, in this chapter, the research which has been done, and the services available for children experiencing domestic abuse, are briefly discussed in order to provide a basic framework for subsequent considerations about the subjects of this book, the adults they evolve into. Without knowledge of the impacts on children, we cannot hope to understand the long-term impacts on adults. Hence, the chapter gives a short conceptualising introduction to research and policy work related to children.

What we do know is that domestic violence is a common experience for children. In a 2011 large-scale UK study, for example, the NSPCC interviewed 2160 parents or guardians of children and 2275 young people aged 11–17 years. Twelve per cent of children under 11 and 17.5 per cent of those aged 11–17 years had been exposed to domestic violence between the adults in their lives (Radford *et al.* 2011).

Anecdotal evidence

This poem was written for the first author by an eight-year-old boy, Quentin, briefly staying in a refuge.

WHY DO THEY DO IT?

Why do they do it?
My dad hits my mum.
I tell them to stop.
They don't listen to me.

They don't care what I think,
They don't listen.
They just argue.
I can't stand it.

I feel bad.
I feel bad all the time.
I hang my head.

This boy went on to explain his very useful ideas for how he and his mother might fix the situation together. He thought that 'if she could just get a bit stronger', they could get rehoused and manage on their own, and he had practical ideas for how he himself could help her strengthen herself in this way, as he longed for. This was his aim, as he took on various adult roles to try to support his mother. The outcome was not good in this instance in that the mother did not manage to 'get a bit stronger' and no one (except, it seemed, the first author, who had no formal position or role in the matter) listened to what the boy had to say. He felt overlooked and frustrated, and he could not understand why no one heard him and why his views and carefully thought-out solutions were ignored. He and his mother left the refuge and went back to the man and to more violence, disruption and upset.

There is much anecdotal evidence of this sort, garnered from refuges and from children themselves about the impacts of domestic violence on children. Adopting adult roles prematurely and inappropriately is clearly one. In the testimony of 'Patrick' (a pseudonym) in Chapter 9, his brother had taken on such adult roles before his time, protecting Patrick in the process. Another boy, a teenager who contributed to the book as an adult, planned a whole new life with his mother's participation, to escape the domestic abuse from his father. In the plan, he was to abandon his life trajectory of going to university, and would, instead, leave school and earn money to support her and his younger siblings, once their father had gone. Their joint plan did not come to fruition, and he carried his sadness, pain and disillusion throughout the next 30 years.

Research on children and domestic violence: only a recent issue

It is not surprising that, as we discuss in the next chapter, there is little research on adults who have experienced domestic violence as children. Until the mid-1990s, there was almost no research on children themselves in relation to domestic abuse. It is a sad fact that the impacts on children of witnessing or living with violence of this type between the adults in their lives have been ignored historically (even after domestic abuse itself began to be recognised from the 1970s onwards).

Gradually in the 1990s, developments began slowly to take place, building internationally on the work of activists and dedicated practitioners. In the UK, the findings of various key Child Death Inquiries which found that domestic abuse should be an issue of child protection concern (O'Hara 1994) were also of significance. One well-known example from the early 1990s was the Sukina Hammond case. The Child Death Inquiry (Bridge Child Care Consultancy Service 1991) reporting on Sukina's death at the age of five years at the hands of her father, found that, had the severe domestic violence being experienced by her mother been taken into account, the death might have been prevented. Instead, it was virtually ignored as a factor.

Agencies tended at the time to overlook domestic violence in child protection work, and the impacts of living in a domestically violent household for children were little known. In North America, a variety of early studies had noted that children who had been exposed to domestic violence were 'silent' or 'forgotten' victims (Elbow 1982; Rosenbaum and O'Leary 1981; see also Edleson 1999). When the issue of children and domestic violence first began to emerge in the 1990s, mainly in Western countries, key US researchers John Fantuzzo and colleagues suggested that: 'research on children who witness family violence is a special case of counting the hard-to-count and measuring the hard-to-measure' (Fantuzzo et al. 1997, p.121). In the UK, it was as late as 1995 that Elaine Farmer, in research for the Department of Health, could still write, in relation to child protection, about the striking disregard of domestic violence in cases of child abuse and the 'missing link' between the two (Farmer and Owens 1995, p.223). However, things were beginning to change.

Considerable research on child witnesses was developed from the early 1990s in Canada, where the work of Dr Peter Jaffe and his colleagues in London, Ontario, has been of key importance (see, for instance, their seminal book, *Children of Battered Women* (Jaffe, Wolfe and Wilson 1990), or, for a more recent example, Jaffe, Baker and Cunningham 2004). Research on the experiences and needs of children who witness and grow up with domestic violence was slower to get going in the UK, but has developed substantially in the last 15 years or so (while related research on their subsequent lives as adults remains thin on the ground). Since the mid-1990s, UK activists, social care practitioners and women's groups have campaigned widely around the issue of children and domestic abuse (Hague *et al.* 2000; Hester *et al.* 2007), and awareness among practitioners and agencies has begun gradually to increase.

Attention to the issue accelerated through the late 1990s and 2000s, and, in most of the rest of this chapter, we consider the subsequent UK research specifically, with reference to other countries only on occasion. The titles of texts which may be of use to practitioners or researchers are noted. For example, in 1994, Audrey Mullender and Rebecca Morley published the first book in the UK on children and domestic abuse, called *Children Living with Domestic Violence* (Mullender and Morley 1994), an edited collection with key contributions including an important early analysis of the possible inter-relations between child abuse and domestic violence by Liz Kelly (Kelly 1994). Various studies began to be undertaken at about the same time, the first being conducted by NCH Action for Children and called *The Hidden Victims* (Abrahams 1994). This study found that 80 per cent of children in the domestically violent households in the study had been severely affected, according to their mothers, and 13 per cent had run away *purely* because of the domestic violence.

These pioneering pieces of work were followed by various others including a comprehensive NSPCC study by Caroline McGee, published as *Childhood Experiences of Domestic Violence* (McGee 2000), which looked at children's and women's experience of domestic abuse and of service provision. A further study was one of only 22 in the national Economic and Social Research Council's Children's Research Programme in the 2000s (Mullender *et al.* 2002). This research found that children in general want to be informed and educated about domestic violence, and that child victims would like to be involved in finding solutions, where this can be achieved safely. Two books came out of this study, *Children's Perspectives on Domestic Violence* (Mullender *et al.* 2002) and a book in children's own words, *Stop Hitting Mum!* (Mullender *et al.* 2003).

Particularly important texts in looking at issues for children experiencing domestic violence between the adults in their lives began to appear in the UK from 2000 or so, drawing on the insight that domestic violence is an abusive context for children to grow up within. Two of these are the key general overview book, *Making an Impact: Children and Domestic Violence*, now in its second edition (Hester *et al.* 2007), and *Domestic Violence and Child Protection: Directions for Good Practice* (Humphreys and Stanley 2006). A 2011 research review, *Children Experiencing Domestic Violence: A Research Review*, provides a useful overview in this context (Stanley 2011).

Impacts of domestic violence on children

Now, in the second decade of the 21st century, domestic violence has finally been recognised as a child protection issue in the UK, and most relevant agencies have policies and strategies in place to which practitioners need to refer and which they are required to follow. However, recent studies have noted that the impact of domestic violence on children is still not always properly understood within child protection and children in need services – even now (Farmer 2006; Hester *et al.* 2007; Mullender *et al.* 2002).

The considerable literature that has grown up in the last few years generally agrees that the impacts on children are complex and cannot be reduced to lists of 'symptoms'. They may include becoming more aggressive or more withdrawn; bed-wetting; distress; depression; suicidal thoughts and actions; school problems; behavioural difficulties; becoming overly protective of mothers; taking on inappropriately adult roles; and pain and distress as adults. There is no hard and fast evidence in the UK literature of particular impacts that always occur. In other words, the experiences of child witnesses are multi-faceted and the effects on them are hard to predict (Hester *et al.* 2007).

What is clear, however, is that a wide range of children's developmental outcomes are likely to be compromised by exposure to domestic violence. A Canadian meta-analysis of international studies on the effects of children's exposure to domestic violence by David Wolfe, Peter Jaffe and colleagues (Wolfe *et al.* 2003) identified impacts on social, emotional, behavioural, cognitive and general physical health functioning across all the relevant research. The team looked at 41 studies for the meta-analysis, and 40 of these indicated that children's exposure to domestic violence was most particularly related to emotional and behavioural problems. However, Wolfe and his team found that there are relatively few empirical studies with adequate controls and with a sound theoretical basis. With this note of caution, it is still possible to identify some common experiences for children.

In the previously noted Hester *et al.* (2007) review of the subject in the UK, produced with Women's Aid, the NSPCC and Barnado's, the authors, including Marianne Hester, Nicola Harwin and Chris Pearson, usefully list some of these specific impacts of domestic abuse on children, paraphrased as follows:

- being protective of their mother and siblings emotionally, and also in terms of intervening, getting assistance, or hiding information if they perceive this to be of help

- attendant physical injuries through, for example, trying to intervene or getting caught in the incident and accidentally injured

- being very advanced in maturity with a possibly over-developed sense of responsibility

- aggression and anger towards the mother, father, step-father or others

- introversion and withdrawal

- feeling guilty about everything

- feeling you are to blame

- self-blame more generally, self-pathologising and bitterness

- being secretive, silent and unable to talk about it

- fear, insecurity and tension

- sadness and depression

- truanting and running away

- school difficulties

- disruptions in schooling or in living arrangements, accommodation, etc.

- poor social skills

- alternatively, highly developed social skills and high achievement

- similarly, the ability to negotiate difficult situations

- emotional confusion in relation to parents

- bed-wetting

- nightmares and sleep disturbances

- eating difficulties and weight loss

- developmental delays on occasion

- social isolation

- difficulties trusting others.

Some of these impacts clearly may endure into adulthood and are further discussed in later chapters.

On the other hand, it is also important to be aware that children may recover admirably well, so it should not be assumed that harm is automatically an outcome in all cases (Mullender *et al.* 2002; Radford and Hester 2006). Thus, crudely making such an assumption can amount to pathologising children and overlooking their resilience, their sometimes heroism and their ability to be social actors in their own lives and to solve problems. Some American estimates, for example, suggest that more than half of children (55%–65%) may show no adverse affects (see, for example, Hughes, Graham-Bermann and Gruber 2001). We clearly need to avoid 'the misuse of dramatic, generalising descriptions of child witnesses of domestic violence, of stigmatising this group of children' (Peled and Davis 1995, p.110), while also taking a positive approach in terms of the protective factors or influences which may lessen the impact of domestic violence and make the child more able to resist its adverse effects. Children do grow up to be well-functioning adults despite these experiences.

However, while recognising positive and encouraging outcomes where they occur, a large variety of studies now exist which have identified the potential negative impacts of domestic abuse on children (Stanley 2011). For example, in a meta-evaluation of 118 (mainly US) quantitative studies, Kitzmann *et al.* (2003) found significantly worse outcomes compared with those for comparison groups of children who had not witnessed domestic violence. There was a significant correlation between exposure and psychosocial problems. Previously, in 1999, Jeffrey Edleson reviewed over 80 research papers on the issue which identified a wide range of emotional, cognitive and physical problems associated with exposure to domestic abuse (Edleson 1999).

For both heterosexual and same-sex families, impacts on children are known to vary with age, gender, ethnicity and class, but these variations are not straightforward (Hester *et al.* 2007). In other words, in the case, for instance, of gender, some boys become withdrawn (and not necessarily more aggressive as might be anticipated) and some girls become more aggressive (and not necessarily more passive or withdrawn, as also might be anticipated) (Kelly 1994; McGee 2000). Diversity is key: there is no way in which 'one size fits all'. For instance, issues for children from various black and minority ethnic communities will vary, and cultural sensitivity needs to be part of all relevant responses (for example for children of South Asian origin, see Imam and Akhtar, 2005; Mullender *et al.* 2002). Disabled children, or the children of disabled parents, are also likely to have particular issues to address which need to be considered by professionals (see Hague *et al.* 2008).

The interconnectedness of domestic violence and child abuse

Domestic violence and direct physical or sexual abuse of children are known to co-exist in many cases, and domestic abuse between the adults in a child's life is one of the most common contexts of child abuse – and an important indicator of risk (Hester *et al.* 2007). However, it is important to also remember that the gender, power and relationship issues involved between men and women, in both couples and ex-couples, and which lead to domestic abuse, are indeed an adult matter – and usually a gendered one. Thus, there are many cases where domestic violence is a quite different phenomenon from child abuse, and the two do not occur together in such instances (Dobash and Dobash 1992; Mullender *et al.* 2002).

Back in 1995, in the study noted earlier, Farmer and Owen found a co-existence of domestic and child abuse, identifying, in the cases of direct child abuse that they studied, an incidence of domestic violence that was twice as high as the incidence that social workers on the cases knew about (Farmer and Owen 1995). Since then, a wide variety of studies have found significant interconnectedness, varying between 20 per cent and 60 per cent of cases where domestic violence and child abuse co-exist (Hester *et al.* 2007).

In a small but highly significant study back in 1998 by Marianne Hester and Chris Pearson with the NSPCC, one-third of the cases studied involved both domestic violence and direct physical child abuse. What is important, however, is that when staff were trained to monitor for domestic violence, that is, to actually ask whether it had occurred or not, this percentage increased to two-thirds (Hester and Pearson 1998). In a large study on child maltreatment also for the NSPCC, Cawson (2002) collected data from 2869 18–24-year-olds. Domestic violence was reported by 80 per cent of those experiencing serious physical abuse;

by two-thirds of those experiencing serious sexual abuse; and by 88 per cent of those reporting neglect.

Coping strategies

There has been some research work on how children cope with domestic abuse (further discussed in Chapter 6). Many of the protective factors (Rutter 1985) that individuals need in order to cope with trauma are precisely those which may be missing in cases of domestic violence. Protective factors of this type that help children deal with traumatic experiences are known to include: loving and secure relationships with parents; a secure home base; social, school or community involvement; and the presence of friends and of family such as grandparents. All of these might be missing where, for example, the child, albeit with her or his mother, has fled the family home due to domestic violence. (For a discussion of these issues, see, for example, Mullender *et al.* 2002.) The absence of just the factors that might be of help to deal with domestic violence makes it all the more remarkable – and a tribute to the children concerned – that so many cope so well, through painful difficulties.

Some authors on sexual abuse have claimed two types of long-term coping mechanisms. The first is defensive and leads to an ongoing acceptance of, and 'accommodation' with, the abuse situation. In such instances, the person concerned tries to protect themselves and adapt to what is going on. The second mechanism leads to 'resolution' and to a reframing or overcoming of the abuse, resulting in a more positive outcome so that the person can move forward in a new way (Kelly and Radford 1998; Koss and Burkhart 1989). Using this framework, similar reactions and outcomes have been identified for children experiencing domestic violence (Mullender *et al.* 2002). Attempting to move towards the second 'resolution/reframing' outcome could be an important strategy for children exposed to domestic violence, for professionals working with them, and for their later adult selves.

In the Mullender *et al.* (2002) study, children often used simple but effective ways of coping to deal with their experiences of domestic abuse, both in terms of internal processing of these experiences and through using external approaches. Coping strategies used by children in the study could include finding a 'safe haven': for example, a quiet place to gather themselves before going to school, or a haven in the mind to which to escape. Talking to a grandmother or trusted adult (either about the domestic violence or about quite unrelated, supportive topics) was often a successful way to cope, as were hiding, trying to get help, or bonding strongly, perhaps cuddling up, with siblings. Indeed, sibling support could greatly improve the possible outcomes.

Thus, the complexity of understanding the issue involves reflecting, not only on the impact of the abusive experience itself, but also on a variety of mediating factors and of coping strategies (Edleson 1999). Child witnesses of domestic abuse have been found to use coping strategies which are both emotionally- and problem-focused (Peled 1993; see also Folkman and Lazarus 1980). Thus, as for other forms of abuse, children's resilience in these upsetting situations is a key resource for professionals to work with. This is particularly the case in terms of dealing with distressing personal impacts, developing autonomy and confidence, and being involved in – or having a stake in – solutions (Grotberg 1995, 1997; Mullender *et al.* 2002).

The Mullender *et al.* research found that it is vital that children, as social actors in the situation in a variety of ways, have some agency in what happens to resolve it, wherever possible. Although such attempts had often been entirely overlooked by the adults involved, as for Quentin, whose poem started this chapter, children in this study talked openly about grieving, worrying, formulating plans, and attempting to take responsibility for their mothers and siblings and overall for seeking out solutions. This type of involvement might mitigate in favour of improved outcomes for the children when they reach adulthood.

Contact after separation and domestic violence

All the UK research on children and domestic abuse that has been conducted so far has found high degrees of contact (both informal and court ordered) with abusive fathers, and has identified concomitant risks of further violence to either mothers or children (see, for example, Hester and Radford 1996; Humphreys 2006; Saunders and Barron 2003). In a small study, for example, Hilary Saunders, then the National Children's Office of Women's Aid at the time, examined homicides of 29 children from 13 families killed in the context of post-separation contact or residence (1994–2004) (Saunders 2004; see, also, Saunders and Barron 2003). Domestic violence was involved in at least 11 of the 13 families, and, in several cases, the children were viewed as not being at risk of harm, even when the mother was known to be facing potentially lethal violence. In all of these cases, one or more children later died. Many professionals in this study showed little understanding of the power and control dynamics of domestic violence, and did not recognise the increased risks following separation or the mother's starting a new relationship.

There has been much debate about child contact and domestic violence in recent years. Practice is meant to have got better, but the underlying principle must be that such contact needs to be safe for all concerned. There were improvements in the 2000s in terms of the recognition that domestic violence can be a child contact issue, with guidelines being produced (see Sturge and Glaser 2000 for details of contact arrangements and guidance). However, there has been some retreat from these principles in recent years, including through the 2005 Children (Contact) and Adoption Act which reinforced the overriding presumption of child contact with both parents (see Hester 2011). Recent pioneering research on child contact for black and minority ethnic families has found that ensuring positive responses to domestic violence within different cultural and family contexts is still hampered by a lack of knowledge or stereotyped responses on the part of many professionals (Thiara and Gill 2011).

Services for children, domestic violence and child protection

Now that domestic abuse is recognised in public law as a child protection concern, extensive policies and services exist, in contrast to the previous years of neglect. These are discussed briefly here. The Adoption and Children Act of 2002 extended the definition of 'harm' that children may experience to include witnessing the abuse of another (for example their mother), which has contributed to a greater attention to domestic abuse in social work practice with children. However, various studies have shown that, in child protection cases, children's experiences of domestic violence are still overlooked on occasion (Hester *et al.* 2007) or, where they are acted upon, there is often attention to the mother only. Male partners, both perpetrators and non-perpetrators, tend to drift out of the picture and become invisible in the child protection process (see Farmer 2006; James 1994).

A further issue which has been identified in the research is that an overly punitive response can be adopted which may deter victims from reporting. On occasion, such an approach can appear to be a knee-jerk response in which procedures are triggered outside the abused mother's control. Both the process and outcome can then appear to be 'blaming the victim' for 'failure to protect' the children concerned (Hester *et al.* 2007). Studies have demonstrated, however, the difficulty of expecting victims of sometimes extreme violence to be in a position to themselves protect their children, without surrounding networks of support (see for example Radford and Hester 2006). If you are being abused and injured yourself, how can you, on your own, shield children from the same violent abuser? It has been argued that supporting the mother to be safe, where possible to do so (which it may not always be, if she returns to the violent partner), may be the best first step, while of course at the same time upholding the paramountcy principle of protecting the welfare of the children (see for example Farmer 2006; Humphreys and Thiara 2002).

However, such good practice may be undermined by the bureaucratic nature of current assessment procedures, which can contribute to lack of trust between social workers and abused women in regard to work with their children (Stanley *et al.* 2010). There may also be a narrow focus on substance misuse and other issues, where these have occurred, which may obscure the need for domestic violence support (Cleaver *et al.* 2007). Indeed, it could be that social workers themselves need to change how they work on this complex and sensitive issue (Humphreys, Thiara and Skamballis 2010).

Further, it is usually the case that children experiencing domestic violence are not consulted by professionals to a possibly surprising degree, as discussed above (Mullender *et al.* 2002). Good practice is to involve and consult children about the issues they are facing and about possible solutions, wherever it is safe to do so. This rarely happens in domestic abuse cases, however, sometimes, perhaps, because professionals hope children do not know about the violence, sometimes for safety reasons, and sometimes due to possible shyness or lack of confidence on the part of the practitioner. However, recommendations about asking children their views were developed in the Mullender *et al.* study (2002). Materials are also now available to enable better relationships between abused mothers and their children (see Humphreys *et al.* 2006, and Chapter 6). In addressing these various issues, a useful development has been that most relevant agencies in the UK have now developed domestic abuse policies and offer specialised domestic violence training (albeit sometimes brief) to their staff. Both in-house policies of this type, and specialist training offered, need to be reliably and carefully used by professionals working on the issue. Domestic violence training is provided by Women's Aid and other domestic violence specialists, and often then cascaded through the organisation concerned on a 'training the trainers' basis. Further, Women's Aid provides a nationally accredited training qualification for practitioners of domestic and sexual violence services, including specialist independent domestic violence advisers, as well as training for a range of other relevant agencies from health professionals to prison officers. Training for independent domestic violence advisers and for the domestic violence courts that now exist is also provided through an organisation called Co-ordinated Action Against Domestic Abuse (CAADA).

Relevant agencies (for example, the Children and Family Court Advisory and Support Service (CAFCASS), the National Society for the Prevention of Cruelty to Children (NSPCC) and the Home Office) often also now offer domestic violence toolkits. These publicly available toolkits give detailed information on domestic violence and on how to work with victims and survivors. Similarly, the health service offers practice guidance (for example Department of Health 2005), as do relevant children/families and adult care departments within social services in the UK. Practice guidance on working with disabled women experiencing abuse is available (see Hague *et al.* 2008; and also the *No Secrets* guidance (Department of Health and Home Office 2000) which, however, needs to be used sensitively and carefully with disabled women). Thus there are now training initiatives, assistance, practice guidelines and specific domestic violence policies to back up services.

The coalition government, at the time of writing, has developed a *'Strategic Narrative'* on *Violence against Women and Girls*, accompanied by a *Call to end Violence against Women and Girls Action Plan* (Home Office 2011). As a result, strategies on violence against women and girls are being developed across localities (replacing, in the main, the previous domestic violence strategies) and would be expected to include some attention to the children of abused women. Working with both victimised women and children involves a careful process of risk assessment, and protocols now exist to accomplish this. For example, the police and other major agencies use risk assessments conducted through the Domestic Abuse, Stalking and Honour-Based Violence (DASH) Risk Identification, Assessment and Management Model (DASH 2009).

Subsequent work with children includes the ensuring of safety, and the provision of empowering and non-judgemental support and, on occasion, therapeutic counselling. All studies show that safety and confidentiality need to be prioritised as the first considerations (Hester *et al.* 2007). Detailed safety planning work is helpful for both children and women (especially if they remain living with the abuser), and agencies can assist in drawing up such practically based and individually-tailored safety plans. Support groups also now exist, including specialist children's groups to assist children and young people to recover from their experiences of domestic abuse. While ongoing children's groups which work with facilitators on domestic violence exist more widely in North America (and include group manuals and activities, see for example Hague, Kelly and Mullender, 2001), they are sometimes available in local areas in this country, particularly with programmes run by Barnardo's. In some cases, groups for children are run alongside sister groups for the mothers. Children may greatly benefit from participating in such groups if they wish to do so. Group work with children as a recovery tool is discussed in more detail in Chapter 6.

A wide range of specialist domestic and sexual violence organisations now exist (mainly in the third, community, sector) (Stanley 2011), which is an important development. Within these, Women's Aid and domestic violence specialist services have developed a range of services for children affected by domestic violence. The pioneering website, the Hideout (Hideout 2011), run by Women's Aid, is a dedicated website for children and young people in this situation, and there are some other web resources specially for young people. An interactive Message Board for children to use is also operated by Women's Aid (and can be accessed through the Hideout) and is proving to be a valuable resource.

Significantly, refuge organisations can often provide children's workers who work with, and offer support to, children resident in the refuge with their mother. These workers may include both specialised staff offering in-depth support and counselling for children and parenting help for their mothers, and also play and activity workers. They can sometimes also work with non-resident children and provide outreach support, and have developed considerable expertise in child work in a sensitive and down-to-earth way. (For a historical coverage of the development of children's work in refuges, see Hague *et al.* (2000). Direct work with children is also discussed in more detail in Chapter 6.)

These are the main specialist services for child victims of domestic violence between adults, but are sometimes overlooked in child protection and other proceedings. Further, the funding for children's work in refuge and outreach services, and the other resourcing required, have always been, and remain, very insecure. They may be even more insecure in the future. The current cutbacks in public expenditure in the UK, announced from 2010/11 on, may directly threaten these advances. Already, various domestic violence projects have closed, or are threatened with closure, due to lack of funding. But, at the time of writing, we have yet to face the full impacts of new financial strategies, reduced budgets and mandated cutbacks which may dwarf those of previous generations. Specialised children's projects in domestic violence services are likely to be particularly vulnerable to cutbacks and many are currently threatened (Community Care 2011; Women's Aid 2011a). Nevertheless they continue to exist.

Education initiatives are now being developed in schools across both the UK and other countries to educate young people that domestic violence is not acceptable behaviour in relationships (see for example Ellis, Stanley and Bell 2006; also, for London programmes, Thiara and Ellis 2005). This work in many schools, and across the broader education system, teaches about healthy relationships and abuse, and is aimed towards building future generations who will be intolerant of domestic violence. A forthcoming book on this work in the UK, again by Ravi Thiara and Jane Ellis, will shortly add greatly to available knowledge on such educational programmes in schools (Thiara and Ellis forthcoming). These may take the form of education packs for classroom activities and lessons, or school workshops and discussions. Further, some inter-agency groups of children's services now exist across the country, which bring together agencies specifically to improve local responses to children experiencing domestic abuse. Thus, there are possibilities for helping today's children avoid some of the damaging effects of childhood domestic abuse that often have an adverse impact on the adults they later become.

This very brief review is intended just as an overview and, among the research studies and service provisions available, mainly in the UK, it has only identified some of the principal ones (see also Stanley 2011). However, for the benefit of practitioners, in Chapter 6 practical ways of working with children facing domestic violence within child protection and other contexts are discussed in detail. Thus, there are some ways forward in enabling children and young people to mend from the long-term impacts of domestic abuse and to build fulfilled lives. But what of people who experienced domestic abuse as children and are already adults?

Chapter 3

Scarcely an Issue at all

*Research on Adults who Experienced
Domestic Violence as Children*

This chapter reflects on what research exists on the impacts for adults, both men and women, of witnessing domestic abuse as children. Sadly, it appears that there is very little at all in the UK, although there is more in North America, where in the US specifically, a number of studies, often quantitative surveys, have been conducted. In the UK, however, there are scarcely any, coupled with very few dedicated services. The issue of the impacts of domestic abuse on people once they have grown up has tended to escape public, academic and agency scrutiny.

There are, however, a variety of personal biographies and testimonies. The NSPCC in the UK, for example, publishes an extensive list of published biographies of this type, in its publicly available booklists. A few blogs also exist on the issue, together with a small number of dedicated user-led websites, recovery handbooks, and some counselling and therapy possibilities. Ways to deal with and to work on this issue for both adults and practitioners are discussed later in this book. The discussion here is, rather, about the long-term effects of childhood domestic abuse in specific terms of the research available. The chapter is presented as an overview, and not as an in-depth academic analysis, although it does contain multiple references to a wide range of academic literature. For those wishing to skip such material, the subsequent chapters present personal testimonies and insights from survivors, gathered for this book.

Diversity, transcendence and adjustment

What do we know, then, from the existing research evidence base, about the lasting effects of childhood domestic violence on adults? As discussed in more detail later in this chapter, we know that they vary widely. We also know that an understanding of diversity and difference is of key importance in addressing them. Diversity in responses and life experiences is likely to include such factors as the person's gender, cultural and class background, ethnic heritage, degree of poverty or wealth, lifestyle, disability, health and illness, sexuality issues, interaction (or not) with service providers, parenting and how as a child he or she was brought up, community and family support, and so on (Women's Aid 2010). We know the possible impacts range from lifelong trauma to almost total adjustment and the development of a fulfilled life. Some people manage to avoid subsequent distress, both without help, or after transforming self-development or counselling. Thus, there is a wide variety of ways to deal with, move beyond or transcend childhood experiences of domestic violence, and some routes to recovery are discussed in Chapter 8.

As one example, in Utah, Linda Skogrand and her collaborators describe the experiences of 90 survivors of traumatic childhoods to give, in the author's words, a 'silver thread' of hope through transforming stories of how to survive. Their 2007 book, *Surviving and Transcending a Traumatic Childhood: The Dark Thread*, examines experiences of childhood trauma and abuse, including exposure to domestic violence, and how some victims have dealt with their life situations to endure and overcome them, in a compelling guide to transcending adversity. The title identifies the heritage of abuse in childhood as a dark thread which often winds its way relentlessly through the lives, aspirations and emotional journeys of survivors, sometimes resurfacing when least expected.

This text, and others like it, document the endless challenges facing children and adults with abuse experiences as children, including domestic violence, and examine the proactive coping strategies and the development of resilience that may have made their recoveries a success. Thus, there are clearly possibilities for change, personal growth and development, and for a 'moving beyond' the impacts as adults. It is also clear that adults are not necessarily adversely affected. Nevertheless, many are damaged and traumatised. So what are the features of such damage and trauma and how can the research help? As there is not a great deal of literature specifically on the impacts of domestic violence experienced by children on the adults whom they later become, particularly in the UK, one way of addressing the issue (as in the Linda Skogrand study above) is to draw on, and learn from, the large amount of more general research on the impacts of wider childhood maltreatment and abuse. This wider body of research clearly cannot be relied on for specific findings about childhood exposure to domestic violence, of course, and may also address children's experiences that might be experienced as more deeply abusive, such as serious child sexual abuse. It would then be inappropriate to extrapolate findings falsely. However, some insights about the impacts of domestic abuse experienced as children can be gleaned from the general literature, if utilised carefully and with measured judgement. Thus, the research on maltreatment is discussed here in some detail.

Research on child maltreatment and subsequent adult difficulties

General studies on the impacts of maltreatment and neglect as children on subsequent adult lives show that sometimes these impacts remain largely dormant, only to emerge at key times in later life (McQueen *et al.* 2008). This may, similarly, be the case for childhood domestic violence. Further, abusive experiences in adulthood can reopen old wounds of past child abuse or neglect that may lead to further adverse outcomes for adult survivors, and this may also apply in cases of domestic abuse experienced as children.

In fact, research on the impacts of wider maltreatment and abuse in general has increasingly, in recent years, specifically included exposure to childhood family violence as a named sub-category, alongside other categories of 'neglect', 'emotional abuse' and so on. Thus, the five main types of child maltreatment (in the American literature at least), are generally now considered to be: physical abuse; sexual abuse; emotional maltreatment; neglect; and witnessing domestic violence. However, lumping many types of abusive experiences together under one heading of 'maltreatment' in this way is clearly un-nuanced, and potentially misleading, and could lead to erroneous findings, as we noted above, but even so the general research on maltreatment, carefully used, can provide a helpful starting point to show us the right direction.

For some adults, then, the effects of child maltreatment and neglect are chronic and debilitating. But for others, the research confirms the anecdotal evidence that more positive outcomes are possible, despite painful childhood histories (Miller-Perrin and Perrin 2007). People can sometimes rise above childhood adversities, and it is worth emphasising this.

Difficulties are strewn across the terrain, however. Everett and Gallop (2001) describe how experiences of childhood trauma can lead to overwhelming emotions. These emotions can include:

> Anger, sadness, guilt, and shame... Coping mechanisms can become over-generalised with time and, without protective factors (i.e., positive events or characteristics) to intervene, these

negative outcomes may continue throughout life. Adult survivors of childhood trauma may also find it difficult to control emotions and/or actions. For adults with a history of childhood trauma, recollections of past trauma can almost be as strongly felt as if it was happening again. (Everett and Gallop 2001)

The authors explain that these adult recollections may result in unexpectedly strong reactions that may surprise the person concerned. These could include emotional lashing out in anger or bursting into uncontrolled weeping in response to minor events (Everett and Gallop 2001). Rage that is denied expression at the time of the abuse may re-emerge years later, sometimes in inappropriate or frightening ways (Doob 1992). Such general observations about the impacts of childhood trauma can also be seen to apply in some cases of childhood domestic violence.

The large body of general research shows that many victims of maltreatment and abuse of all types experience a range of long-term effects into adulthood. For example, in terms of emotional abuse, including witnessing domestic violence, Dorota Iwaniec and colleagues have examined risk and resilience, and identified numerous ways in which such experiences are likely to enhance vulnerability to negative outcomes. Emotional abuse can be seen in their studies to lead to children failing to thrive, for example at school or in terms of friendships, and to emotional 'stunting' in adult life (Iwaniec, Larkin and Higgins 2006).

One of the most common reactions to all types of childhood abuse, if not *the* most common, has been widely identified as depression, which can play a debilitating role in the life of the later adult. Depression related to earlier abuse is often severe and may be endured throughout adulthood. It is frequently coupled with anxiety (Bohn and Holtz 1996; Kaplow *et al.* 2005). In one American representative study, for instance, adults who had experienced child neglect and abuse were two and a half times more likely to have major depression, compared to adults who had not had these childhood experiences (Afifi *et al.* 2009).

A multitude of other emotional and psychological problems, trauma and difficulties in adulthood can also be seen, from the literature, to result from childhood maltreatment and abuse, including gastrointestinal problems, stress, nightmares and repetitive upsetting dreams (Bohn and Holtz 1996; Lang *et al.* 2004). Most widespread perhaps are feelings of lack of self-worth, hopelessness and inability to settle happily into adult life and relationships, with attendant sexual and interpersonal problems, and marital and relationship dysfunction. A watershed event in the field, especially in North America, was the identification of post-traumatic stress disorder (PTSD) as a set of symptoms experienced after a traumatic event, including sometimes as a consequence of child maltreatment and abuse (Briere, Kaltman and Green 2008; Herman 1992; McCloskey and Walker 2000). This connection was particularly highlighted in the key work of Judith Herman (Herman 1992; Herman 1997), further discussed later.

Related impacts may include self-harm, suicidal impulses and suicide. Gladstone *et al.* (2004), for example, looking specifically at child sexual abuse in a sample of adult women, found that abuse of this type led to life-long self-harm (often extreme), suicidalness, severe depression, and further exposure to personal violence post-childhood. Revictimisation as adults is a finding of this and other studies on general maltreatment and abuse, and includes the victim perhaps experiencing later sexual and physical assault and exploitation, and prostitution. Similarly, risky sexual behaviour, teenage pregnancy and eating disorders have been identified among older adolescent girls with abuse experiences as children (Boyer and Fine 1992; Herman, Russell and Trochi 1986).

In the US, the very extensive Adverse Childhood Experiences (ACE) Study used a large data set of nearly 14,000 adults, and identified a very wide range of health consequences of childhood adversity, including poor physical health, autoimmune disease, frequent headaches, depressive illness, multiple health-related quality of life issues and risky behaviours (see, for example, Anda *et al.* 2006; Dube *et al.* 2001; 2002; Edwards *et al.* 2005: Felitti *et al.* 1998). Further outcomes for all types of child maltreatment that have been identified include living in fear, extreme nervousness, avoidance of medical professionals on occasion (Leeners *et al.* 2007), and substance misuse (Freyd *et al.* 2005). Similarly, Wekerle *et al.* (2006) have presented an overview of knowledge regarding the impacts of childhood maltreatment which included depression, trauma, emotional and behavioural problems, and, importantly, mental health difficulties.

There is considerable literature on the link, specifically, between maltreatment and childhood trauma in general, and later diagnosed mental health issues. Everett and Gallop (2001), writing as in most of the above studies in an American context, for instance, highlighted the difficulties of relying on retrospective memory as a source of information, as further discussed below. However, these authors identified a strong inter-relation between adult mental health problems and abuse as children, and went on to elaborate helpful interventions by professionals, including practice guidance and models of treatment.

Mental health impacts are likely to be complex and may be experienced as inter-related with other problems. In a recent meta-analysis, Hilberg and colleagues found a clear association between child sexual abuse and adult mental health difficulties across all the relevant studies, although effect size varied widely and significantly (Hilberg 2011). A study by Banyard, Williams and Siegel (2001) examined exposure to multiple trauma in terms of child sexual abuse and subsequent adult mental health outcomes. In this study, childhood abuse led to lifetime histories of complex, multiple traumas. The study pointed to the importance of understanding the intermeshed nature of trauma exposure for many survivors (see also Banyard *et al.* 2008).

Confirming such findings, many researchers have advised caution, and alluded to the need to develop a nuanced understanding of the extreme complexity of the impacts of abuse and the outcomes in adulthood (for example Briere *et al.* 2008). Briere and Jordan (2009), for example, suggest that the multiple psychological effects of child maltreatment and trauma are too complicated to fit into a single framework or syndrome. They note this complexity in the connections between psychological outcomes and multiple contextual variables such as social marginalisation and poverty, as well as childhood maltreatment, confirming the findings of Banyard and her colleagues, and others, as above. Trying to make simple statements about these issues would be misguided.

The impact on adults of domestic violence as children is far less researched, even in North America, but the materials about general abuse and trauma have some purchase, and victims may have similar responses and find that they experience some emotional resonance with the findings of this type of research. Nonetheless, the absence of specific material is striking and concerning – in the UK context at least. As we have noted, there is more research in North America on the issue, which is further discussed below. But some of the main reasons for the lack of specific research are the difficulty, methodologically and ethically, of actually doing the studies.

Research problems: retrospective self-reported evidence

Some studies on later impacts of early abuse use retrospective methods and rely on reports by the people concerned, looking back to the past, and this tends to be particularly the case for studies of the later impacts of childhood domestic violence. All such research methods are prone to difficulties, but it can be argued that these difficulties can particularly be the case for something as varying, hidden and complex as the long-term effects of experiencing domestic abuse as a child, as compared with some other forms of direct abuse and maltreatment.

One of the problems can be that almost all of the research on adult survivors of domestic abuse tends to depend on self-reports which may be uncorroborated by any third party or independent source, so that they, in general, are not a very solid source of data. A related major difficulty is the reliability of any retrospective studies on earlier trauma (see for example Krinsley *et al.* 2003; Widom and Morris 1997). Retrospective recalling of events long in the past is known to be sometimes unreliable in providing trustworthy research evidence, although good practice does exist, including the development of particular and complex statistical and other techniques for data collection and research analysis (Clements, Oxtoby and Ogle 2008). Further, a rejection of such methods out of hand, as in accusations of 'false memory syndrome' for some adults recalling sexual abuse as children, would be neither propitious nor wise.

Overall though, researchers using methodologies which rely on retrospective accounts (for example, those of adults with mental health problems looking back on their childhood and remembering incidences of domestic violence) may find it hard to ensure that their studies are robust pieces of research – and that they are viewed as such in the field. People's memories may be fragmented and selective, sometimes without the person concerned even realising. Particularly in terms of teasing out specific and replicable connections between cause and effect, retrospective studies can thus not always be depended upon. Prospective studies (where study participants are revisited in the future to find out what happens in the long-term) can be conducted, of course, and sometimes are (see for example Ehrensaft *et al.* 2003). This type of prospective research clearly takes a very long time, is prone to drop-out over the period (possibly especially for abuse and trauma survivors) and is subject to a variety of logistic difficulties. Kendall-Tackett and Becker-Blease (2004) have argued that there needs to be a mix of prospective and retrospective studies, as both types of research can provide insight into the long-term consequences of child abuse and neglect.

A further difficulty of conducting such research is the possibility of re-traumatising the victim years later. It has been suggested that research participants may have adverse reactions after the research, and that fear and distress may deter such participants from speaking out during research interviews, leading to falsely low rates of disclosure of earlier abuse (Briere and Jordan 2009; Krinsley *et al.* 2003). However, there is also research evidence that such re-traumatisation is rarely the case. For instance, studies by Walker *et al.* (1997) and Becker-Blease and Freyd (2006) have discussed the ethics of asking about abuse, and the harm of instead adopting a 'don't ask, don't tell' policy. They found that respondents viewed participation in retrospective studies positively, and that it was unlikely that direct questions about childhood abuse, used sensitively, led to deep trauma (especially if the issue had previously been ignored and minimised by helping agencies). Such questioning could sometimes lead to immediate distress at the time, but could also be part of recovery, of feeling respected and 'listened to', and of beginning to address the past, especially, perhaps, for something as overlooked as domestic abuse witnessed in childhood.

These and other researchers have also noted the danger of over-emphasising the vulnerability and weakness of adult survivors of trauma, and have suggested that such a research perspective can be unethical and stigmatising, re-silencing victims (Becker-Blease and Freyd 2006). Thus, these authors propose that retrospective research of this type is possible with safeguards, and with careful attention to good practice and to avoiding both bias and revictimisation by the researchers. Such research now takes place for other types of childhood trauma as indicated above. But rarely, it seems, in the UK at least, for adults traumatised by domestic violence in childhood.

Where are the studies on domestic violence specifically and what do they tell us?

The answer is that it is not easy to find them, certainly in the UK. However, a variety of mainly American studies have found direct impacts. (Some of these studies are dedicated to the issue of domestic abuse, and, in others, the topic forms one dedicated section of a wider study of abuse.) Back in the late 1990s, Jeff Edleson identified long-term effects of childhood exposure to domestic violence as associated problems of the original abuse (Edleson 1999). Also, in the 1990s, long-term negative impacts of domestic violence were found by a few other research teams. Murray Straus, in one of his many studies, has reported how childhood exposure is a risk factor for life-long problems among a nationally representative sample of American women and men (Straus 1992). Indeed, it has been suggested by some North American researchers that one of the most deleterious phenomena to which children can be exposed is violence between their parents or caretakers at home (Briere and Jordan 2009).

In an article entitled 'Adult daughters of battered women: resistance and resilience in the face of danger', Anderson and Danis (2007) discuss how living in a home where there is domestic violence for a child is to live in an environment of fear and powerlessness which is likely to lead to adult adversity.

Depression, suicidal impulses, ongoing sleep disturbance and mental health problems

As for other types of abusive experiences, depression, self-hatred and lack of self-worth have been discussed in the research literature as particularly trenchant and long-term impacts of witnessing domestic violence. Silvern *et al.* (1995) identified depression, and also low self-esteem among female – but, interestingly, not male – survivors, as well as other trauma-related symptoms for both men and women college students. In a further early study, Henning *et al.* (1996) found, in carefully controlled research, that women who had been exposed to domestic abuse as children experienced more distress and impaired social functioning, compared to those who had not been exposed. These impacts may include suicidal impulses and suicide attempts, connected to feelings of desperation, self-hatred and lack of self-worth. Impacts for those who have witnessed family violence are often persistent, distressing and ongoing.

One impact which has been strongly identified is sleep disturbances which may endure throughout life and have potentially debilitating effects for both child and women victims. In the UK, Pam Lowe and colleagues have presented compelling evidence of how sleep management is often embedded in the social context of domestic violence. Adult women who had been exposed to domestic abuse as adults spoke of having learned to be constantly 'on guard' in case of violence (Lowe, Humphreys and Williams 2008). For children, this hyper-vigilance may develop throughout their young lives, so that they are likely, on an ongoing basis, to watch out for arguments and fights occurring between parents or carers, often in order to try to intervene. Being 'on guard' in this way may mean that they learn to wake up quickly and frequently, and children may then carry this vigilance and sleeplessness through into their adult lives.

Even when adult women with domestic violence experiences were asleep, the Lowe *et al.* study found that the quality of their sleep was fragile, leading to exhaustion, feelings of inability to cope and ongoing health problems. Confirming this study in terms of childhood exposure, sleep difficulties have been identified in other studies as a specific outcome in adulthood of experiencing intimate adult violence as children (Mertin and Mohr 2002; Mullender *et al.* 2002). Upsetting arguments and possible violence between parents or caretakers tend particularly to take place at night, when children are in bed and when they may be at a life stage where they especially need their sleep in order to be healthy while growing up. Disruption and attendant fear and distress at night may thus be especially difficult for a child, and may then become an engrained habit for the future.

Witnessing childhood violence as part of multiple abuse

It can be hard, however, to separate and identify specific impacts of domestic abuse experienced as children. In the Henning *et al.* (1996) study, noted above, for example, the authors stressed that it was difficult to isolate the impacts of childhood domestic violence from other factors. This difficulty has had an impact on many studies. Exactly what causes what is hard to ascertain, especially where the adults concerned have experienced combinations of indirect or direct abusive or neglectful experiences in childhood, or where life experiences have been otherwise complex or traumatic.

Nevertheless, as discussed above in terms of general childhood maltreatment, complex associations have been identified between different types of direct and indirect abuse. For example, connectivities between witnessing intimate partner violence during childhood, child abuse, women's later health, adult domestic abuse exposure, and health care use were examined by Cannon *et al.* (2010). Poor health status, higher prevalence of depression and of experiencing domestic abuse as adults, and greater use of health care and mental health services were observed in the women participants who had witnessed intimate personal violence during childhood, as well as those who had experienced direct child abuse, compared with women with no exposures. Significantly in this study, women who had witnessed adult violence, but *not* experienced child abuse themselves, had comparatively worse health and greater use of health services.

In another study by Feerick and Haugaard (1999), the subjects were college women who completed a questionnaire about experiences of intimate violence both in childhood and adulthood, and connections with adult adjustment and relationship functioning. Witnessing marital violence was associated in the study with childhood physical and sexual abuse, and with both mental health risks and physical assaults by strangers for adults. Women who had witnessed marital violence as children also reported more symptoms of post-traumatic stress disorder than other women, after family background and abuse variables were accounted for (as further discussed below).

As would be anticipated, impacts on adults tend to be more severe, in the findings of the research literature, where exposure to childhood domestic violence had occurred alongside actual child physical or sexual abuse. For example, among people who had experienced all three of these forms of violent childhood experiences, the risk of later revictimisation or perpetration has been found to be increased 3.5-fold for women and 3.8-fold for men (Whitfield *et al.* 2003), and this issue is discussed in more detail in the next section. Sousa *et al.* (2011), in a longitudinal study of the long-term impacts of child abuse and witnessing domestic abuse, identified anti-social behaviour in the late adolescence of participants. They found that multiple exposure resulted in increased impacts which overlapped and compounded each other.

In the UK, Daniel McQueen, the late Cathy Itzin, Roger Kennedy, Valerie Sinason and Fay Maxted, all UK writers, researchers and activists, have produced a book, named *Psychoanalytic Psychotherapy After Child Abuse: The Treatment of Adults and Children Who Have Experienced Sexual Abuse, Violence, and Neglect in Childhood* (McQueen *et al.* 2008). The result of a broad collaboration, the book draws on insights from psychoanalytic psychotherapy to map the very wide-ranging and intersecting impacts of different types of childhood neglect and abuse, specifically including experiencing domestic violence. The book was produced for practitioners, therapists and psychiatrists, and its practical and therapeutic insights are also noted in Chapter 8. It identifies, in a UK context, a very wide range of poor physical health outcomes and other deleterious consequences for adults who were abused as children, including directly through domestic violence exposure, which together form a complex, overlapping overall picture.

Verbal conflict and aggression

Teicher *et al.* (2006) looked at childhood maltreatment as a psychiatric risk factor in later adult life, and specifically included verbal aggression and conflict between parents, as well as witnessing domestic violence and other types of abuse. Verbal conflict in the study had strong impacts on children and on the adults that they later become. Again, exposure to multiple forms of maltreatment had an effect-size that was often greater than the sum of the components. Combined exposure to verbal abuse and witnessing domestic violence had a greater negative effect, according to some of the measures used, than exposure to familial sexual abuse. This somewhat surprising finding indicates what a strong effect verbal aggression between parents can have on children. The authors identified inter-parental verbal aggression as a potent form of child maltreatment.

Revictimisation and passing the violence on

There is conflicting evidence as to how much childhood exposure may be related to adult experiences of abuse, either as perpetrators or as victims. Academic analyses have been produced, looking at the various sides of the argument in more detail than is possible in this brief overview. As a few examples, in a survey of research studies by Kwong *et al.* (2003), it was suggested that all forms of childhood exposure were predictive of adult abuse. Ehrensaft *et al.* (2003) found, in a prospective study, that such exposure was a good indicator of later adult perpetration of victimisation. However, a meta-analysis of 160 studies where domestic violence was in some way named as included alongside other sorts of abuse found that the connection was only weak to moderate (Stith *et al.* 2000). Some scholars have spoken of the direct inter-generational transmission of abuse in the specific context of domestic violence. However, the effect size is often small in these mainly quantitative American surveys. The widespread and often uncritical adoption of such a strong word as 'transmission' (in relation to witnessing domestic violence specifically, rather than to direct child abuse) is likely to be ill-advised and distorting of the actual facts.

It has been found that women who have experienced or witnessed parental violence could be at risk of being victimised as adults, as noted earlier, as they are more likely to have low self-esteem and they may have learnt that violent behaviour is a normal response to dealing with conflict (Mouzos and Makkai 2004). Further, experiencing intimate partner abuse between their adult carers as a child could lead to adverse outcomes a generation later for a woman's own children and the way she is able to parent them, according to some studies (see for example Dube *et al.* 2002).

It cannot, of course, be denied that childhood experiences clearly affect adult life. However, how much domestic abuse itself is passed on across generations remains a moot point (Hester *et al.* 2007; Radford and Hester 2006). The evidence is contested and contradictory. Outcomes can be different, for example, if the original parents or parent substitutes remain together or divorce, with intact families of origin, where the perpetrator has stopped being violent, being sometimes a predictor of less later violence in the lives of the grown-up children (Moon 2000). Some researchers have suggested that the literature has overestimated the role of witnessing domestic violence as children in causing abusive experiences in later life, and underestimated the importance of other factors, for example, poor parenting (Capaldi and Clark 1998). Similarly, experiencing domestic violence may co-occur with other social difficulties, for example poverty and substance misuse, that may influence adult values and ways of behaving (Fife and Shrager 2011).

The issue is clearly a complicated one. In summary, there is some evidence that experiencing domestic violence as a child can sometimes be a predisposing factor for later experiences of adult abuse and sexual victimisation, and this possibility should not be overlooked by service providers. On the other hand, many who have been exposed to violence as children live lives as adults in which they are not further abused. The issue appears to be altogether more complex than any simple association. Conversely, it is certainly the case for adult domestic violence victims that very many have not been witnesses of domestic abuse themselves when children (Hague and Malos 2005).

For perpetrators, rather than survivors, the issues are, of course, somewhat different. Some studies do find that male perpetrators are more likely than non-perpetrators to have grown up in domestically violent families (for example Rosenbaum and O'Leary 1981) and there is particular evidence in the American literature. Feldman, for example, proposes that childhood exposure to violence in one's family of origin is one of the most consistent correlates of the later perpetration of adult domestic violence (Feldman 1997). It has been suggested in one research study that 30 per cent of boys exposed to inter-parental violence will grow up to be violent themselves (Margolin and Gordis 2000). While this is an upsetting figure, it would still mean that 70 per cent will not grow up to be violent.

Thus, in sum, it can be seen that it is true that some people who witnessed domestic violence as children go on to become either abusers or victims themselves. But it is also true that for many people this is not the case. Men who witnessed violence against their mothers may grow up to be committedly non-violent, whereas there are plenty of adult abusers who did not experience or witness abuse in childhood (see for example Hague and Malos 2005; Mullender et al. 2002). Living within societies where violence is feted in popular media, and where patriarchal relations in terms of men's frequent power over women exist, have been widely suggested as a broader way of understanding intimate personal violence by many men, whether or not they have had childhood abuse experiences (Hague and Malos 2005; Kerley *et al.* 2010; Sugarman and Frankel 1996). Perhaps we need to make sure we do not fall into easy or un-nuanced solutions.

Various researchers directly corroborate this suggestion, pointing out that we need to avoid simplistic assumptions about any direct connection between childhood experience of domestic abuse specifically and adult perpetration or victimisation (for example Stith *et al.* 2000). It is possible to recognise that experiencing violence is indeed traumatising and that the outcomes for individuals will vary widely, without imposing a rigid conceptualisation of cause and effect.

Childhood domestic violence and post-traumatic stress disorder

As for general child maltreatment, there are a few studies that identify ongoing effects of childhood domestic violence that are broadly similar to classic post-traumatic stress disorder (PTSD) where the original trauma returns in a variety of guises to haunt the sufferer. For example, childhood domestic abuse exposure was found to be a significant predictor of adult PTSD in a study by Kilpatrick, Litt and Williams (1997). Similarly, McCloskey and Walker (2000) found a connection between experiencing family violence and later PTSD. While PTSD is less used as a diagnosis in the UK than in North America, it still has purchase in this country and can be useful in understanding the possible depth and long-lasting nature of the personal impacts (Radford and Hester 2006). Post-traumatic stress disorder can sometimes be acute, and often consists of ongoing anxiety, panic and emotional trauma. It can reoccur long after the precipitating trauma, and endure throughout life. It does not require much imagination or thought to understand that PTSD is likely to be particularly distressing where the precipitating trauma occurred right inside someone's own family and home, and when they themselves were impressionable children (Herman 1997; Jaffe *et al.* 1990), thus magnifying possible adverse outcomes. Judith Herman in her ground-breaking work, further discussed in Chapter 8, elaborates this concept to 'complex PTSD' in cases of personal abuse and trauma.

PTSD symptoms may include (in summary) numbness, detachment and withdrawal, impaired concentration, hyper-alertness, jumpiness, flashbacks and severely disrupted sleep patterns, possibly long term (see also Brandon and Lewis 1996; Hendricks, Kaplan and Black 1993; Hester *et al.* 2007). However, it is a confusing picture. While the studies noted above found a positive association between witnessing childhood violence and later PTSD, some others do not. In an Indian context, Kulkarni *et al.* (2011) found that, while childhood violence exposure plays a considerable role in the development of deleterious outcomes in childhood and adulthood, experiencing family violence in itself, without any other factors, did not necessarily lead to adult PTSD. Kaplow *et al.* (2005) identified pathways through which sexually abused children may develop later PTSD symptoms, but the evidence is less clear for childhood exposure to domestic violence.

What is important for this consideration is that all of these outcomes, to varying degrees of severity and in varying combinations, are common for survivors of domestic violence as children and can lead to ongoing difficulties throughout adulthood. In the next chapter, the specific impacts of childhood domestic abuse on adults are discussed in more detail, not in a research context, but instead drawing on the words of survivors themselves. Their often moving insights have been drawn from the findings of a focus group of survivors, from interviews, from the testimonies in the book, and from other empirical research, and build on the more academic-oriented discussions in this chapter.

Chapter 4

The Impacts of Childhood Domestic Violence on Adults

What Survivors Say

The following poem is by a woman in her 40s regretting the loss of her childhood through exposure to domestic violence between her parents.

I CAN'T FORGET
I can't get better
I can't forget
Or if I do
It jumps back again.

Go away.
It wasn't fair.
It was my only childhood.
My only one.

Damaged and hurt,
It was the only childhood I had.
I can't have another chance.
That was it.
And you made it a nightmare.

I can't get better.
I can't forget.
It wasn't fair.

This chapter builds on the previous chapter on research findings and what the academic literature can tell us about adults, both men and women, exposed to domestic violence as children. One thing this literature has made clear, as discussed in the last chapter, is the complexity of the issue. There are no hard and fast impacts. Not only do people react as adults in widely varying ways, but witnessing abuse between parents, parent substitutes or carers, as children, may often occur in tandem with other types of abuse. Further, various protective factors and life events are likely to mediate outcomes, and it is hard to separate the effects of abuse from, in any case, the often mixed-up nature of wide-ranging and complex childhood experiences.

Impacts and outcomes may also vary by gender for women and for men in complex ways. For both, they can be equally traumatising and upsetting, although, as noted in the previous chapter, Silvern *et al.* (1995) found that men's self-esteem is sometimes less damaged than women's. Impacts may also vary in same sex families or across differences of ethnicity, class and culture. Overall, the chapters on research findings have given us some pointers as regards these complex outcomes, within the understanding that this book is not aiming to be an in-depth academic treatise on the issue. Rather, as discussed in Chapter 1, the book melds research, practice guidance, testimony, poems and the views of survivors. Here, we listen to the voices of people with childhood domestic abuse experiences and tease out some common impacts.

Raising voices and breaking silences

In Chapter 1, 'Kate' contributed a moving poem about her experiences of domestic abuse as a child, commissioned for this book. Here, her poem continues:

FOR KATE, THE PAST WON'T GO AWAY (CONTINUED)

[I]
Kate feels that she needed to have nurtured
a safe secure place inside her
when she was still young

but she didn't.

She couldn't.
No.

It wasn't possible in all that,
to be honest.

But she feels that she failed yet again
in that –
as well as everything else.

No safety inside, then.

Yes.
Another failure,
her fault again.

[II]
The tears come easy to Kate,
the churning stomach,
the feeling of having no right in this world.

She can't find the solace.
She can't find any foundation,
that real sure place

deep inside
where it should be.

Other people seem to have it.
Kate's isn't there.
No.

Her place,
deep inside,
is fractured and messy

instead of steady
and resilient.

See, she's wrong yet again.

The tears come easy,
the churning stomach.

The feeling of having no right in this world.

Learning from the actual voices of victims/survivors in order to provide authentic evidence has a long history in the social sciences, from Foucault's work with prisoners and others, to standpoint theories, to ethnographic research methodologies, to the 1989 UN Convention on the Rights of the Child (see variously, Aris, Hague and Mullender 2003; Foucault 1972; Harding 1987; Merrick 2006; Mullender *et al.* 2002). In this book, for one of the first times ever, the voices and views of adults with childhood experiences of domestic violence are presented, as part, in this case in particular, of a long line of contributions from the women's movements of the world.

One of the principles of much feminist-inspired activism and research on violence against women since the 1970s has centred on raising the voices of those who have been abused themselves (including victimised men), empowering victims to speak out and viewing their insights with respect and belief (see, for example, Dobash and Dobash 1992; Hague,

Mullender and Aris 2003; Kelly 1988). The women's activist movements have been intent for the last 30 years to break silences, to bring the painful reality of many women's lives into view and to build a better world for women and for children.

Combating violence against women, specifically, has been a major focus of women's activists and campaigners all across the world as part of this wider struggle. Over the years, the silences around gender violence, which those of us in the UK who grew up before the changes of the late 1960s and the 1970s will recall, have been systematically broken. So it has been with domestic violence against women. So it has been with child sexual abuse. So it has been with the impacts of domestic abuse on children. So it has been with rape and adult sexual violence, including rape in marriage; with forced marriage; with violence in black, minority ethnic and refugee (BMER) communities; with honour-based violence; with same sex violence; with intimate violence against disabled women... The list is endless.

Each silence, each hidden women's issue, has been slowly and painfully brought to light by women's activists and campaigners, by feminist researchers, by women's groups and groups of survivors, by grieving relatives and by dedicated practitioners (see, for example, in general: Hague and Sardinha 2010; Herman 1997; Kelly and Radford 1998; for disabled women: Hague *et al.* 2008; for children: Mullender and Morley 1994; for same sex relationships: Donovan *et al.* 2006). The authors of this book, with many other feminists, have been part of breaking the silences, of nurturing the painstaking social change to which raising previously hidden voices gives rise.

It is, and remains, an honourable procession of hard-fought-for causes, in the true and right meaning of the word 'honourable'. Breaking silences for adult survivors of domestic violence (both women and men) is part of this great procession. In this chapter, then, the voices of victims and survivors are the focus, as they are in the subsequent testimonies in the rest of the book.

Gaining the evidence

The insights elaborated here on the impacts on adults of domestic violence witnessed in childhood are derived principally from the discussions and suggestions in the testimonies, poems, interviews and an in-depth focus group conducted by the main author. For the latter, six women (aged 22–61 years, with childhood experience of domestic abuse and from a range of different class and ethnic heritages and sexualities) joined the author in these discussions which lasted for over three hours, with various further subsidiary discussions. All agreed to take part and signed consent and confidentiality protocols. Group members also kept notes on their experiences and thoughts over two weeks, and shared these. All were also provided with support and contact lists for helping agencies, if requested, and were presented with small thank-you gifts. The outcomes of the focus group have been further developed with data from a number of qualitative interviews (15) with women who have had childhood exposure experiences, including women from BMER communities. These interviews were conducted with the same safety, consent and confidentiality provisos. This qualitative data is melded with insights from the poems and testimonies and the outcomes of other small-scale research conducted for this book.[1]

The issues raised by the interviewees and members of the focus group (which have been divided into different sections in the rest of this chapter) often overlap, repeat and reinforce each other, frequently also repeating and reinforcing the research findings discussed in the last chapter.

The impacts vary hugely

The outcomes of the focus group and interviews demonstrated that impacts vary widely and that cultural, ethnic and class backgrounds, individual histories, parenting style in the family of origin, country of upbringing and so on were clear factors. Growing up in an extended or joint family could helpfully mediate what happened, although it could sometimes make it worse according to two interviewees of South Asian origin. While often severe for both genders, impacts tend to vary if you are a woman or a man, and they also seem to vary by age. Being brought up in the 1950s or 1960s when domestic violence was not on public agendas was likely to give rise to different outcomes for adults than growing up in the 1990s when domestic violence had begun to be recognised as a public, rather than just a private, issue. Across the spectrum of backgrounds, however, including country and community of upbringing, economic and class positioning, issues for BMER families, and so on, there were also clear and moving similarities. Participants (including both women and men) found that they shared many common experiences and impacts. At the same time, alongside the similarities, the later effects in adulthood of

1   This data provides useful insights gained directly from survivors, but does not represent the robustness of a full research study or large-scale survey.

childhood domestic abuse varied in terms of extent, from very little or no impacts to very serious outcomes, as discussed in more detail in the rest of the chapter.

This discussion is intended as a catalyst and pointer for subsequent analyses and research. The chapter represents a beginning, a breaking open of a rather disregarded subject and a 'first-time' vehicle for expression among mainly silenced victims. What the survivors said is powerful and compelling. Service providers, agencies, therapists, activists and researchers need to listen and take stock.

Issues that the focus group members identified

The focus group members were all women, but many of their insights apply to male victims too. In general, focus group members and interviewees were broadly in agreement about the detrimental effect that childhood domestic violence had had on their lives. They identified the many facets of the pain and ongoing difficulties that their childhood experiences had caused. Particular issues identified by one member usually turned out to be common with at least some of the others. The focus group discussion was lengthy and emotionally draining, but ultimately an uplifting, experience for all. Participants said that they had found it helpful to talk with others and to find out that they shared so many common experiences, and that it had been a supportive event. All agreed that the outcomes were cathartic despite the distressing personal histories being shared.

Focus group members and other interviewees broadly agreed about and identified the following range of (sometimes overlapping) impacts in their adult lives (with the quotes taken directly from the words of various interviewees):

- feeling not worth anything
- being 'self-destructive in all sorts of sometimes subtle ways'
- feeling to 'blame for everything in life'
- finding it 'hard to be happy even when you are'
- feeling angry and it 'bursting out, sometimes extremely, because of otherwise having to keep it inside like you learned as a child'
- weeping easily, and often inappropriately
- 'You get upset too much: it's hard to be emotionally "continent"'

- finding it difficult to 'own the good and successful things you achieve', to recognise and honour your own life and achievements
- experiencing abuse as an adult, 'often subtly, not necessarily the big stuff'
- only feeling worth anything if you are 'giving out to others, otherwise feeling useless'
- not feeling you have had the chance to develop a 'core'
- always seeing the negatives, rather than the positives, in any situation
- repeatedly feeling that you let everyone down and 'always messed everything up'
- being constantly depressed or anxious
- not sleeping, including both being awake at night and sleeping lightly to awaken easily
- feeling inferior to almost everyone and in almost all situations, 'even ones where you are clearly the expert'
- being generally miserable in everyday life
- sabotaging your own happiness
- resentment at the loss of how childhood ought to have been
- not having a chance to develop as a fully integrated person 'because the adults took up all the space when you were a child'
- not being clear about personal boundaries
- being ambivalent about close or intimate relationships
- sometimes having difficulties with sexual relationships
- engaging in sexually risky behaviour, not feeling that your body is worth protecting
- taking ill-advised risks, in general
- hiding issues and silencing
- telling lies to protect everyone from abuse
- being manipulative to avoid conflict and possibly violence
- self-pathologising

- self-harm 'in both big and small ways'
- having mental health issues and having to use the mental health services
- being suicidal.

This is a devastating list. Those who have experienced domestic violence as children may find reading such a list rings bells, is distressing, or touches on previously obscured personal issues. Getting support is key in such situations. Talking about and possibly resolving such personal difficulties can be of help, and ideas for doing so are discussed in Chapter 8.

Not being too badly affected perhaps

Nevertheless, negative impacts are not universally experienced. Before discussing the various painful issues in the above list in more detail, it is perhaps helpful to acknowledge that it is possible, as noted in the last chapter, to survive childhood domestic abuse fairly well as an adult, and this was confirmed by our informants. From both the research literature and the narrative discussions that inform this book, it is completely clear that some people who witness domestic abuse as children seem to be able to lead happy, fulfilled lives as adults, more or less untouched, throughout, by the violence of their childhood, and resilient to later life traumas and problems. Indeed, their childhood experiences may have 'toughened them up' (interviewee) and enabled them to deal effectively with later difficulties.

Why then do some people emerge without much anguish? From the interviews conducted, it emerged that a substantial factor could be the experience of being shielded by other family members from the full impacts. Some children are effectively protected from upset and damage, especially by an older sibling or parent. Not being the oldest child can sometimes help, according to our respondents. For example, our testimony-giver, 'Patrick', movingly describes (in Chapter 9) not being too badly affected himself as the second child, while his older brother had carried scars, anguish and a sense of failed responsibility throughout his life. Several interviewees similarly described how some of their own siblings had managed, in the words of one group member, to avoid 'carrying the weight of it'. In her case, she surmised that the negative impacts on her and the protective stance she had adopted had somehow freed her siblings from damage.

Between them, our interviewees described various further issues as possible explanations. They suggested, and the research on resilience discussed both previously and in later chapters confirms, that positive outcomes are more likely if the person concerned has certain personality traits, for example, good-humouredness, self-confidence, a relaxed attitude, or choosing not to delve into the emotional parts of life. Some people, they also suggested, may have left their experiences behind in a long out-distanced and almost forgotten past that does not impinge on their separate, adult selves. Some may not remember – they may have no conscious memories at all of previous domestic abuse in their lives. Some may be able to shrug off what happened to them as water off a duck's back. Others may feel, our discussants pointed out, that it was not something that was a true part of 'them' but rather to do with their parents/carers, and so not part of their own life, trajectory and self-image. They may, therefore, remember if pushed, but in general never think about it, dwell on it or reflect on it.

It is worth noting that there are likely to be millions and millions of people with these childhood experiences in the UK alone, given the high level of domestic violence among the population in this and other countries, as discussed in Chapter 1. National surveys in the USA have found that between 11 per cent and 20 per cent of adults report witnessing intimate partner violence as children (Briere and Jordan 2009; Henning *et al.* 1996; Straus and Smith 1990). Self-evidently, not all of these manifest damage from the experience. It is clear that many adults may well be able to sail on, regardless. Thus, it is possible to manage life moderately unscathed – and many people do.

On the other hand, getting on with life seemingly untouched may come at a cost, as discussed in the focus group. For some people, there can be repression, emotional inarticulacy and inability to include feelings – and crucially an addressing of them – in one's life view. Outward cheerfulness can disguise traumatic experiences that remain hidden and possibly perilously repressed, and may need or demand to be addressed at some point in a life. It can suddenly become clear that being a seemingly balanced or unemotional person is a more fragile thing than previously thought. Past unaddressed pain can erupt unexpectedly.

Ongoing pain

Overall, then, it is true that there are many who forget, transcend, repress or appear unaffected by childhood exposure to intimate personal violence between the adults in their lives, and focus group members recounted real-life examples of this happening. But there are many, many survivors of childhood domestic violence who are deeply affected and who go on to experience ongoing distress, guilt, pain and diverse problems, as our informants testified. According to the focus group members and interviewees, and confirming the research findings discussed in the last chapter, these impacts can extend to extreme trauma, and sometimes mental health difficulties and suicide. We know that people very often suffer deeply, but many may try to carry these childhood traumas inside themselves secretly and painfully. They may avoid seeking help, perhaps from a sense of shame and guilt, and because, like the testimony-givers in Chapters 5 and 7, they were trained as children to hide the domestic violence they had witnessed as an embarrassing and incriminating secret. Further factors might revolve around the fact that there are so few services.

Our respondents talked about how victims might also feel that they do not want to make a fuss, or be possibly tarnished in others' eyes by exposing their experiences. They might feel they should be able to deal with their feelings on their own, and battle in private with their memories and anguish. This had been the lived experience of several of our informants. They movingly explained how scars and damage abound, across the adult psyches and lives of people with this painful personal history. In the next sections, particular manifestations and overlapping impacts described by focus group members and interviewees are further elaborated in more detail.

Feeling that you are not worth anything and do not have the right to a full human life

Several of our informants expressed strong feelings of worthlessness, sometimes connected to guilt, self-blame and still feeling that they had to hide the details of their home lives, even as adults. They spoke (as, of course, survivors of many types of abuse do) of feeling guilty and wrong about everything, as further discussed below. The group members described both blaming and feeling disgusted with themselves as adults, because of their childhood experiences and of it having become habitual to conceal experiences. All the members agreed that these feelings developed out of their lives as children, in terms of trying to disguise and manage adverse experiences by internalising them deep inside themselves, with attendant psychological problems later. They alluded to literally 'swallowing' their experiences so as not to let others know, so as not to expose themselves to possible criticism or voyeurism from friends and family and, originally, so as not to let their parents or carers down in public. Several said that, because of their childhood experiences, they felt wrong about everything they ever did, as did the authors of the most of the poems in this book.

They suggested that their childhoods had set them apart from the 'proper children' who did not have to hide parental conflict and abuse. Their childhood friends had not had to deal with such issues, they supposed, although maybe, in reality, some were secretly doing so also. Several focus group members said that they were further set apart by trying to protect their mothers, sometimes intervening to stop the violence, often failing to do so, becoming desperately upset in the process, and maybe being hurt themselves. The poet, 'Juliette', who produced the poem which began this book, 'Arms outstretched to them', talked of trying to intervene, of 'the feeling of the shades coming down'. She spoke of begging both her mother and father to try to stop but being overlooked, not being able to influence what happened, feeling hopeless – and still feeling so, even after 40 years:

> But she couldn't stop it,
> crying and sobbing,
> arms outstretched to them.

Attendant to this type of life experience as children, further emotional impacts which focus group participants identified included associated fear, guilty distress and pain for themselves and their abused parent. Watching one's mother being hurt by one's father or father substitute or carer, and being powerless to prevent it, to save her, had led directly to adult feelings of helplessness, failure and worthlessness. The impact of such a situation for young and vulnerable children is perhaps too painful to be fully or accurately imagined by people without such experiences.

Lack of self-esteem

Thus, feelings of lack of self-esteem, of always being in the wrong, of being not worth anything, were common to all the interviews. Two women explained that:

> You feel worthless and as though you are made of rubbish.

> I treat my body like a dustbin – because I'm just a pile of sh**. It doesn't matter to me what I put in it, I regard it similarly to putting things in a garbage chute. I know that I am not worth anything, however hard I try.

One result of such experiences for interviewees had been that they felt wrong about most things, not just sometimes, but all the time, and felt that they could be relied on to 'mess everything up' in the words of one of the women quoted in the list above. One of the interviewees stated that:

> It's the survivor thing again, because you're a survivor, you always make a mess of it. You do well and then you sabotage it. I don't mean you mean to sabotage it, you just do.

She felt that her childhood experiences had 'hard-wired' her for failing, spoiling things, letting herself and others down.

Some participants spoke of only being able to find solutions to lack of self-worth by becoming 'rescuers' themselves, by giving out to others, and being able to feel like a full human being solely when so doing. If they were not giving to others, they felt that they had no right to exist and were 'otherwise feeling useless' as another woman quoted in the above list put it.

Thus, in summary, lack of self-esteem and feeling that you are worth nothing as a person linked strongly, for the survivors interviewed, with issues of self-blame, feeling responsible for the violence experienced, guilt and fearfulness. They also identified becoming secretive and manipulative because of hiding the secret of domestic violence as children. Several described hiding events and emotions – even when those events and emotions were not related in any way to the conflict and violence at home. What might then happen was having to manipulate subsequent events to achieve the concealment, as the interviewees below suggest.

> I tried to hide it all when I was a kid and I still try to hide things often which gets me into difficulties of trying to manipulate things or having to fib. I have to constantly struggle against that to make sure I don't do it – the manipulating thing...

> It's only making up things for good things, to keep things even though... not destructive lying. I feel that I am responsible for keeping everything good and hold myself to blame for nearly everything. (Two focus group members)

This second interviewee felt that she was responsible for 'keeping everything good', 'keeping things even', clearly beyond any one person's responsibility. Being overly responsible, coupled with being extremely self-critical, were common experiences, as discussed in the next section.

Being overly responsible and often achieving highly

Some of the literature on child witnesses of violence concentrates on poor educational outcomes and achievement difficulties, and some addresses the experience of looked-after children in the child care system who may have multiple problems in adulthood. Such outcomes may indeed be the case for adults who experienced childhood domestic abuse. However, the interviewees in this study had not been in this situation. Rather, as the above quotation from a focus group member demonstrates, they had tried, sometimes inappropriately, to take a great deal of responsibility for everything, had perhaps been used to holding adult responsibilities since childhood and had in some cases become very high achievers themselves. Several had been model students and employees, always trying to prove themselves, to overcome their feelings of worthlessness and to manage life to avoid possible conflict and violence.

One university colleague spoke of never feeling worthy and always feeling inferior even when her expertise was unquestioned by anyone else. While this can be a common feeling for women, it appeared to be hugely amplified for this interviewee and for others with similar histories.

> I can feel inferior and blame myself at all times over everything, if it rains, if the bus doesn't come, if a paper of ours comes back for revisions, if I get two negative evaluations of teaching among 89 excellent ones. Ridiculously – see there I go again – I am a respected academic and a PhD examiner and I feel inferior to the PhD student usually and have to force myself not to!
>
> If there is ever anything bad to agree to in terms of my behaviour or actions, I agree immediately; if there is ever anything good, I ignore it and attribute it to others.

While such emotional responses are by no means confined to abuse survivors, they may be accentuated in these situations of childhood domestic abuse, especially where the former child may have lacked all power and purchase in relation to the adult conflicts and domestic violence in their lives, so that they may have felt helpless, at fault and in the wrong. The adults they later become are likely to also have such feelings. As a child, they may have felt worthless because they could not fix the domestic violence, because they lived a childhood life of guilt or shame, because they assumed a mantle of responsibility and then (as a child dealing with adults) were not able to live up to it. They then carried these feelings into adulthood. Therapists and counsellors would be better able to theorise about and to explain these behaviours in more depth. They were, however, common across the interviewees, focus group members and others consulted for this book.

Depression, anger and anxiety

The participants had often felt depressed, coupled with omnipresent feelings (as noted throughout) of self-blame and lack of confidence which reinforced the depression and negative feelings. As discussed in the previous chapter, the most common long-term effect of abuse of any type is depression. With the exception of one or two, this was the case for all the research informants and testimony-givers. Some spoke of long-term depression. Others described feeling, as an adult, that life was grey and a struggle, and that this way of regarding the world was something that they had learned unconsciously in childhood. Always being on guard and often experiencing damaging or distressing events, instead of more joyous childhood pursuits, had long-term impacts in terms of not being able to enjoy life fully. The poet who began the book spoke of 'bitter, and a tangled feeling' and of this feeling enduring and enduring – 'even though she's well past 50'. Two other interviewees spoke of 'getting down' at the least possible opportunity, even when there was objectively nothing to be depressed about. One spoke of being depressed as her 'default position', all other things being equal. Being slightly worried, miserable, depressed and watchful had become her modus operandi.

Other emotional responses which focus group and other individual informants and interviewees had experienced included recurrent anxiety which had scarred their lives. They also spoke of becoming irrationally angry on occasion due, they suggested, to pent-up anger held inside possibly for years since childhood, and of recurring desperate crying. Re-emphasising what focus group members said in the list above, emotional outcomes could thus include: first, feeling angry and it 'bursting out sometimes extremely, because of otherwise having to keep it inside like you learned as a child'; and second, weeping easily, and often inappropriately. 'You get upset too much: it's hard to be emotionally "continent"' (two focus group members).

Sleep disturbances

I STILL CAN'T SLEEP AND IT WAS 20 YEARS AGO

I dreaded finding broken furniture,
I dreaded my father getting angry and upset,

when I came home from school
better not invite my school friends in, just in case.

As I got older
there was never a meal without arguments.

And I'd always feel sick
And tried to reason with them both,

with him.
'Please don't, please stop it, please, please,
please...'

I used to jump up at night to intervene.

To try to stop it.
I'd listen all night.

I didn't let myself sleep deeply.
Always on the alert.

I still can't sleep
And it was 20 years ago.

This poet, 'Juliette' (pseudonym), also contributed the poem which began this book. Here, she continues her contribution, suggesting, like our testimony-giver 'Anna', that sleep disturbances are very common following childhood domestic violence, as we discussed in the previous chapter in terms of research findings. She explains that she quite deliberately taught herself not to sleep, resulting in sleep difficulties throughout her life.

In more detail, domestic violence often occurs at night and children commonly learn to stay awake to watch out for it and train themselves to sleep shallowly and vigilantly. Sleep difficulties of this type could endure long-term, according to our informants, as engrained patterns of behaviour, and thus might include both being awake at night and, even when sleeping, doing so particularly lightly to awaken easily as an adult. Because of both factors, recuperative rest was likely to be insufficient and this insufficiency could become chronic and a long-term adult situation, with possible resulting health issues.

> I used to view each night as me being like Prometheus, pecked by the eagles, or whatever the story was. I learned to wake up instantly, to respond with the fight/flight mechanism straight away in the middle of the night. Rather than being sleepy on waking, I was ready to fight or flee and then not to go back to sleep but listen. So you can see how hard normal sleep would then be. I would end up aching and emotionally fragile. I'm better now a bit. (Interviewee)

Confirming Juliette's stories and the discussion above, this interviewee helpfully explained how either having to be awake or, if asleep, having to leap from sleep immediately (rather than to wake up gradually), ready to flee or fight, means that peaceful rest is scarcely possible. For children having such experiences, possibly alone in their beds and frightened, it can be seen that the pattern could become embedded while they are young and vulnerable, and thus become hard to address as an adult throughout their subsequent lives.

Not taking care of yourself

Some participants had found that, because of the type of feelings they had of not being worth anything and being depressed, they had not accorded themselves, their bodies or their lives the respect that they should have done.

> I don't always think that I should protect myself and that I'm worth whatever it is – so I let things happen to me that I shouldn't... I'll do anything anyone asks because I don't really count. (Focus group member)

Lack of self-care of this type could lead to risky behaviour, and occasionally to further sexual and other abuse. One of the participants had indeed suffered later sexual abuse. While victims are not to blame for the abusive behaviour of others, she explained how she had put herself in risky, or even slightly dangerous, situations because she did not feel she deserved any better, as further discussed in the next section. This kind of feeling was described both by the focus group participants as above, and also in several of the poems and testimonies.

You don't know what your personal boundaries are: vulnerability and victimisation

Along similar lines, many abuse victims record having difficulties managing boundaries. 'Levine' (pseudonym) speaks about these difficulties in a short poem she wrote for this book (with the collaboration of the first author), using the third person, as 'Kate' did in her poem in Chapter 1.

BOUNDARIES ARE HARD FOR HER

She's called Levine,
a fine name.
But she's not fine.

Boundaries are hard for her.
Because she is only like rubbish,
after all.

That's how she feels.
It doesn't matter
what happens to her, does it?

Inside,
the raking hurts,
the past sneaking up

suddenly
behind relaxed
happy times

and pouncing
to strafe her.
The empty gaps,

the aching memories.
She treats her body like rubbish.
Doesn't matter what anyone does to it, does it?

Boundaries are hard for her.
She's called Levine,
a fine name.

But she's not fine.

'Levine' built on her poem to say (in her subsequent interview) that she did not think she was worth anything and literally treated her body like a 'garbage disposal unit', echoing many allusions to being rubbish or garbage from our informants, as in previous quotes. She did not take seriously what happened to her as being important. Thus, she had few personal boundaries. She said that it did not occur to her that her body might be precious and 'hers'. She just wanted to please other people and so she thought about other things if something unwelcome sexually, or otherwise unpalatable, was happening to her, and let it happen. She's called 'Levine', a fine name, she says. But she's not fine.

One of the focus group participants contributed particularly about this point. Paraphrased here are her beliefs about the issue. This survivor of domestic abuse as a child felt that she had now begun to overcome the difficulties and to manage boundaries more effectively. However, she explained that if someone views themselves as hopeless, they might put themselves in unsuitable situations and cross boundaries that are not advisable, as she felt she had done previously. You also might, she suggested, seek love inappropriately or in potentially abusive situations, sometimes confusing love with sex, in order, perhaps, to substitute for a damaged childhood. She suggested that you also tend to feel that others are right and must know better than you (since you are always wrong), so that you should overcome reticence or personal doubts to do whatever they say you should do, possibly including sexually. These sorts of behavioural issues are common for abuse survivors, but have been largely overlooked in the past for the specific group of adult survivors who had witnessed domestic abuse as children.

Relationship difficulties

Several of the interviewees spoke of more general relationship difficulties which they attributed at least partially to childhood domestic abuse and the sort of emotional confusions and complexities discussed above in terms of lack of personal boundaries. They discussed long-term relationships being affected by recurrent distressing childhood memories, lack of trust for their partner, poor personal behaviour, diffuse sadness and depression, sexual difficulties on occasion, getting seemingly irrationally upset, and possible concealment of issues Further, although only the case for a couple of our informants in their personal lives, several identified direct experiences of sexual or physical abuse in relationships and being exposed to dangerous behaviours. It should be noted that impacts on relationships are likely to be complex and multi-dimensional, and to defy simplistic interpretations. Encouragingly, some of the interviewees and focus group members, and all three of the testimony-givers, had found lasting love and committedly supportive and non-violent relationships.

Passing it on

None of the interviewees felt that they had passed on the abusive experience to their own children, although all agreed that some emotional impacts and behaviour patterns could not help but be passed on. Wider negative impacts on interpersonal relationships have been identified (for example for young adults, see Hester *et al.* 2007), and the informants in the focus group and interviews agreed that this could be the case. However, they also suggested that subsequent difficult or abusive contexts could be relatively low-key for an adult survivor of witnessing abuse as a child. These contexts might still be abusive, they surmised, but sometimes more subtly so than, say, for serious child sexual abuse, so that the person might not quite recognise it at the time.

Two of the participants had experienced physically abusive relationships with men, and one of them had been sexually abused, when they were young and closer to the domestic violence of their childhood, but said that they had been able to move beyond these types of relationships as they became older and learned more. One woman with this experience added:

> But you always have to watch out for reproducing abusive things in your relationships with your partner; it's easy to go there without realising it, because of the past.

As discussed in the previous chapter, the research evidence about inter-generational transmission is mixed and conflicting. It is certainly the case that, while it does not occur for the majority, some victims of childhood domestic abuse may go on to be revictimised (or, possibly, to themselves become abusive). However, this was not the case to any great extent for the interviewees in this study, according to their accounts and discussions.

Feeling that your childhood was stolen and that you could not mature properly

Focus group members spoke about feeling that their childhood had been unjustly taken from them, as the author of the poem at the start of this chapter also felt. Instead of the carefree time experienced by some of their peers, they had been worried, anxious, guilty and hyper-vigilant. They may have tried to intervene and protect their mothers and several had sustained childhood injuries in so doing, as noted previously. They had grieved and worried for their mothers, and felt confused about the person who had perpetrated the abuse, perhaps loving them dearly, perhaps hating them, or somewhere mixed up inbetween and changing at different times and in different circumstances. They felt that their precious childhood had been stolen from them.

For these adults, their childhood experiences had led to the lack of a feeling from childhood of security inside, the absence of a 'space' in which to explore their own emotional landscape (as the poet, 'Kate', eloquently identifies). Rather, their feelings and emotional attention had been highjacked by the conflicts and abuse between their adult carers. Some spoke of not being able to complete the growing-up process in terms of satisfactorily separating themselves from their parents and becoming mature and balanced adults. One interviewee described how her parents were always involved with each other in argument and conflicts and, in her words 'facing each other rather than me'. She then adopted this 'position' too, being bound into their couple relationship, and could not get the separate attention and parental encouragement she needed to separate from them healthily. Because she was always involved with them, was always anxious to prevent violence and worried about her mother, she had not been able to attend to her own growing up and become independent.

> It's hard to grow up right. You stay worrying about them and you can stay a child really. It's like when you were a child you had to behave more like an adult and now you're an adult you still behave a bit like a child if you are not careful.

Wise words perhaps: as a child you were forced to take adult responsibilities at least to some extent because of the domestic violence; as an adult, you still get tangled up with behaving as a child because you have not had a chance to separate from your parents properly and become a grown-up person.

Very serious outcomes

Very serious outcomes can result for adults who experienced domestic abuse as children. These can include mental health problems, sexual victimisation, self-harm, suicide attempts and suicide. While three of the interviewees had been suicidal in the past, none was currently. Several had been self-harming as young adults, cutting their arms and exposing their bodies to hazardous substances. This form of self-abuse has been reported commonly for all types of abuse (as reported in earlier chapters). It is less common to see it reported for cases of childhood domestic abuse exposure, and its identification in such instances may be of help to practitioners and counsellors, and also to victims, in trying to understand personal impacts and ways of behaving.

In terms of particularly severe and distressing impacts, including admission to mental health facilities, suicide and extreme self-destructive behaviour, it should be noted that the focus group participants suggested that very serious outcomes of this type are more common for severe types of abuse such as child sexual assault than for witnessing domestic violence. However, this is not to belittle the fact that, for some adults who were child victims of domestic abuse, the outcomes are very debilitating.

> Of course it is serious, it can devastate your life, can't it, you can never get away from the bad feelings but it probably it isn't as bad as what some women have, is it? Like rape or physically being beaten up as a child or having incest as children. It's bad enough though. Don't want to minimise it or make it seem as if it is not a real trauma and really important. It is...

Self-destructiveness, self-pathologising and self-harm are recurrent features of the lives of those scarred as children. Even where these take comparatively less severe forms, they are likely to be devastating to the person concerned.

Getting stronger

Some interviewees and focus group members had continued to feel damaged, lost and worthless throughout their lives to date. Happily, various other participants spoke of having become stronger in recent years. They discussed finding new and loving relationships, enjoying having children, and leaving some of the more negative impacts behind, even while, on occasion, still being traumatised and besieged with flashbacks, memories, anxiety and grief.

> I went to university as a mature student and got a degree and now I'm working in a job I love.

> I left my first husband, he was a bit abusive actually, I didn't know what I was doing then, but I am very happy in my second marriage.

> I started having relationships with women and I have never looked back. I have left all that male abuse behind, it's very gentle and healing.

For the last woman, moving to relationships with women had been transforming. For others, some positive change had begun to happen through other loving relationships or through counselling, and for one, through attending a group. Cathartic discussions and sudden insights into past behaviour and emotions had been of help, as had finding and sharing with others who were in a similar life situation. It is possible to get stronger and to mend, even though the journey may be a long one with both setbacks and steps forward.

In the next chapter, a moving and detailed testimony is presented by 'Rose Wood' (a pseudonym), charting her own devastating childhood experiences and the long journey – into her 50s – of slowly creeping, and sometimes leaping, towards a healthy happy adulthood.

Chapter 5

Finding Hope in a Cold Place and Thriving Against the Odds

Testimony by 'Rose Wood'

1

Many years ago, Gill Hague and I met at a conference organised to promote awareness of domestic abuse, and particularly the needs of children. Gill heard me speak both as a survivor of childhood domestic abuse and as an activist, campaigning – as many had before me and continue to do so today – for services to support women and children affected by domestic abuse, a globally endemic problem.

At that point, Gill asked if I would contribute to this book which she was planning for the future, and I am proud to do so, not least of all because Gill – who was unaware of this – made such a significant contribution to my own understanding and recovery from childhood domestic abuse, as you will see further on in this chapter.

In addition to services for women and children, for me it was also important for there to be services for men. As a young child, I had loved my father deeply, and the emotional loss of him was a source of immense pain. The sense of loss arose as I grew increasingly aware of his abuse of my mother and older brother, and experienced the terrible fear and deprivation his behaviours had inflicted on us. I did not realise it then, and it is only looking back from the vantage point of my mid-fifties that I have some understanding of the struggle, effort, indignation, and the dreadful length of time that it would take for me to reach a place of... how can I put it... perhaps the term inner peace would be appropriate.

But as I write this, I feel my stomach aching, so I know that is not quite right; I was going to write the word acceptance, but what would I accept – it would never be an acceptance of violence, the right of one to control another, of a parent to terrorise and cause mind-numbing pain, and a husband to inflict emotional harm and physical damage on a wife's body and mind. Perhaps I'll settle for the sense of coming to terms with, and making my own kind of peace with my past and some of the worrisome figures and experiences that populated that time.

We won't talk here about soul, or the damage domestic abuse inflicts on this deepest level of our humanity. We won't consider the confusion born of the discrepancy between the teachings of my Sunday School as a child, and what I saw happening in my home, or how a child develops a sense of justice in the unjust world of her family, or perhaps how a child might use her imagination to such an extent to survive her life that, by the time she is an adult, it feels like there is no imagination left. It might feel, then, that all that remains is a reliance on the concreteness of having enough food, clothes, a bed in a safe house and the physical safety of a lover's arms, in order to feel secure and safe and that the past is not going to be repeated.

Keep thinking, thinking, thinking, ahead, ahead, ahead, make sure everything has been thought of, plan and prepare, try hard, so hard, beware of saying or doing anything wrong, because any slip might mean you're like him, or her, slipping into their ways of being and into hopelessness, fearful of the payback, the punishment to follow.

And, the payback for saying the wrong thing could be catastrophic – like the time I stood up to my very drunken father when he arrived home late from the pub and criticised the meal I handed to him which my mother had prepared. He complained because it was a little dry, due to being kept warm for him for hours. I was 11 years old and, although I was usually a quiet, shy child, something welled up inside me to such an extent that it was not possible to remain quiet any longer, and I confronted him about his late arrival which had led to his evening meal not being quite perfect. As a result of this event (to which I will return later), my father ended up in hospital, my mother in prison and we children ended up in a police station before moving to a children's home.

2

How did we get to this point? How could a little girl's statement to her father about his responsibility for the state of his evening meal have triggered such a tidal wave of events, life-changing consequences arising from daring to say something honest and born of injustice?

If only that could have been the only event, it might then have been possible to account for it as an unexpected incident arising out of a father's reduced inhibitions due to the effects of alcohol, and an almost adolescent daughter's rebelliousness. But – of course – it was not a one off – that

incident was one culmination of a whole sad catalogue of events which
succeeded in turning a loving daughter into an undercover detective in
her own home – desperately vigilant and watchful for any sign of tension;
turning her into a covert strategist who – increasingly as she grew older
(we're talking at 9–10 years) and when her father was out of earshot –
would plead with her mother to leave him; who would work out ways of
escaping from her home if violence broke out. I would imagine and plan
opening my bedroom window, carefully stepping onto the kitchen roof,
crawling across, then down the drainpipe and running like lightening
to the phone box at the end of our road, to dial 999 for the police and
achieve rescue. And, of course, in a war zone, no one is neutral – to stand
by and watch helplessly as my father tried to strangle the life breath out of
my mother became an impossibility from the age of around seven years, so
I climbed in between them pushing with my little arms against my father,
pleading with him to 'stop, stop, Dad, stop' – and so I became at a very
early age a foot soldier in our very own domestic war zone. Oh yes, and
a human shield.

I liked to know what was going on. This was preferential to being
upstairs in bed, fearful, heart pounding, unable to sleep or to see what
was happening, though well able to imagine – and straining to hear any
signs of discord, raised voices, pounding against doors, crashing furniture,
doors slamming (you get the picture). So it was fortunate for me that, from
a young age, my mother used to keep me up late, in the hope that, when
he arrived home, this would distract and dissuade my father from violence.
So – remember I loved him – I would be delighted to see my father, would
chat, cuddle up beside him on the sofa and then – if we were lucky and
he fell asleep – would sit looking at him, unwilling to move in case he
woke up because, in my child mind (although I didn't really understand),
I sensed that I could try to stop bad things happening.

On one occasion, my mother sat opposite us and, noticing that some
money notes had fallen out of my father's pocket, she quietly motioned for
me to pass them to her. I solemnly shook my head and refused to do so,
thinking: 'No, this is Dad's money, it would be wrong to take it without
him knowing'. Of course, at that early age, I still loved my father and did
not understand until later that he kept most of the wages he earned for
himself, giving only a tiny portion to my mother to pay for everything
else: food, clothes, coal, rent, everything we needed for our family, him
included. Despite this, he would criticise my mother when there was not
enough money to go round, or he would beat her when she refused to
hand it over, stealing (as I soon came to regard it) money from her when

he ran out of funds for his own needs. My father was unable to put his children or his wife's needs before his own.

I was in my early 40s when I heard that my father had died. At first, my emotions were confusing. I had walked away from him a very long time ago and had not seen him since my late teens. Yet, the news of his death left me feeling all at sea, with surging waves of feelings that created inner turmoil. To my rational mind, these feelings seemed out of place. After all, I had previously chosen to walk away from, and subsequently grieved the loss of my father who I had loved intensely as a young child, and so long ago. I finally resolved that – irrespective of whatever had gone before – he had been a significant person in my life, both for what he was and for what he had not been as a father, and that it was OK for me to have whatever feelings arose. I realised it was also OK not to understand them – always a hard thing for someone like me to accept – not understanding. Knowing what something meant in order to predict what might happen next was immensely important to me. In fact, survival depended upon it for a child like me who lived in fear throughout her childhood of her mother being murdered by her father.

I did not feel any need or desire to go to my father's funeral. Then, one beautiful sunshine-y morning, about two weeks after he died, I was driving to work when I suddenly experienced what I can only describe as a complete and all pervading sense of liberation, as though something – a burden – had been lifted from me and replaced with a sense of freedom, of joyful, peaceful – liberation is the only word for it. I felt complete, my body felt whole and complete, no sense of any pain or confusion. And, then, it hit me – I realised that what I was feeling was due to the relief that my father was dead. The relief, oh my... the joy, the relief. I scanned myself emotionally to check – and found no sense of guilt attached to the immense feeling of peacefulness and relief that he was now dead. No sense that I was a bad person for feeling this way, this totally unexpected emotion that left me feeling everything more intensely: the sunshine's warm, bright light, the stunning vividness of the greenery of the trees, the sensation of the steering wheel in my hands as I drove along feeling ten tons lighter now that he, my father, was dead.

No longer did I have to be bothered about what I would do if he turned up out of the blue at my door, how I would feel turning him away, denying him access to his grandson, denying my son access to his grandfather and the knowledge of how he looked, denying the possibility that my father might have changed for the better, not wanting to take the chance and not wanting my son to be contaminated by his grandfather's distortions of our past. No more worries about any of that, no more fear, no more self-questioning, no more self-torturing about any of the decisions I had made, including to walk away from him. His death was a welcome ending, a relief and a turning point.

How did we get to this point? How did we get to this place where my heart which had once been so full of love and devotion now felt relinquished of an immense burden that had cast dark shadows over my life, so ingrained that the extent of it could not be known until the threat was removed?

The first time he hit my mother, I now know, was around her head as she held me in her arms, a baby, only a few weeks old. As an older child and well into adulthood I would find myself flinching if a sudden unexpected sound or movement occurred nearby. Such is the impact of repeatedly witnessing someone you love being repeatedly abused – you don't have to be hit yourself to experience terror. Such is the impact of being woken repeatedly in the middle of the night to run to the nearest public phone box to call the police; it can put you on automatic guard, unconsciously expectant, alert for action, ready to avoid danger (or sleep), or to head directly into danger to protect your mum because to lose your mum would feel like the end of the world, like your own death, a catastrophe to be avoided at all and any cost.

3

I recall myself as a young child climbing into my parents' bed and snuggling down happily between them. These were the two people I loved most in the entire world, I felt safe in between them. I adored my father. As soon as I was old enough to do so, I would go to the end of the road on which we lived and sit on the pavement waiting for the first sight of him at the bottom of the hill, eager to catch that first glimpse of him returning from the night shift at the steel mill. Within a few short years, I would grow to dread the first and any sighting of my father. Neighbours once commented on how the colour had drained from my face upon his unexpected arrival at our home, during one of my parents' numerous separations.

I recall my first day at school and all the pleasure this opened up for me. Then – as now – I loved learning and school would quickly become an oasis, a bright place of play, of learning, and of women and men who often showed great kindness, who role-modelled – for the most part –

decency and, in some instances, encouragement, inspiration and hope for the future.

It was the combined efforts of educators and social workers that helped me, particularly those who were prepared to make a personal connection, born of genuine concern for my interests, to reach out, to obviously notice, think about and express their views, including to me – both when I was in danger of going off track and when asserting their belief in my potential and also when stating that it was my circumstances and not me, myself, that was the problem. It was these individuals, with their persistence and steadying faith in my ability to survive and succeed despite the problems I encountered in my family that would help me to eventually build a bridge to a happier future. Indeed, they were the bridge.

The infant school headmistress who listened and gently encouraged my faltering attempts to read and who provided, on at least one occasion, a good quality pretty dress which she adapted to fit me so that I had cause to feel beautiful. The junior school headmaster who provided what was never available at home – the peaceful experience of being read stories to – I can still hear his wonderful comforting voice, delivering stories of Brer Rabbit and Hiawatha which opened up worlds of imagination and places to which to escape and an intense love and commitment to reading as many stories as possible to my own child, and then to those children I've worked with over the years.

The headmaster of my secondary school who was a rock and who, at a particularly difficult time in my life, told me the story of how he came to England in difficult circumstances many years before, not knowing a word of English and only six months before he had to take his 11-plus. If he could learn English in six months and pass an exam dependent upon it, then – he suggested – I could certainly achieve what lay before me. And, because of his encouragement, I did.

The social worker who moved through the hierarchy to a senior position but who fought throughout to maintain casework responsibility for my family, and who was perceptive enough – even though I abjectly rejected the idea at the time – to recognise and state her belief that I would be suited to social work in the future. She was also prepared to be my first referee when – several years later – I applied to become a residential social worker for the very same local authority.

It was these individuals who taught me what it really means to be child-centred in professional practice, and that this sometimes involves challenging the system to innovate, challenging the systemic barriers to providing children who are disadvantaged through abuse, neglect and chaotic family circumstances with what they need in terms of thoughtful, respectful, warm human connection, consistently over time. They also taught me the enduring and life changing impact this can have for those children fortunate enough to benefit and to be able to draw on these strengthening experiences over a lifetime. To these individuals, my heart will never be able to fully express what it holds for them.

To all those currently engaged in working with children in the social, education and health sectors, be under no illusion about the difference you can make in a child's life. You can be that difference. You can be the bridge to a different future and life.

4

I also recall, at four years old, being in a large children's home. Years later, I saw the Children's Services record where it stated that we had been abandoned by our mother. There was no mention of the violence that had driven her away. I do not recall my father visiting, but my mother certainly did. I do recall the pain of her leaving, saying goodbye as I sat quietly on a rocking horse, not moving, immobile, stuck, transfixed and powerless to run after her, or to stop her from leaving, but aching, aching ever so quietly.

We (my brothers and I) returned home. So did my mother, but not until later and after what felt like a long empty eternity to me. There would be more violence and more separations, over and over again. Sometimes, I'd receive a message that mum was at the bottom of the street, and I'd dash off to see her in secret for a little while, fearful of what would happen if my father saw her. I don't recall what or if we spoke – what happened when we were together is obliterated by the awfulness of having to part from her and watching her walk away. And then, so quietly and with a heart so heavy I don't know how it didn't fall out of me, I would walk slowly back up the street to the house that was so painfully lonely without her. On the way home, as I walked past other houses, I have a vivid recall of their stone walls, so strong, so solid, and the contrast between this and how weak I felt as I struggled to put one foot in front of another, not knowing how I was managing this, but somehow my heavy sledgehammer feet moved on automatically, on and into the house. How I would have loved to have melted into that stone, to feel no pain, to be left in peace. There was nowhere to put the pain, no parent who could safely be confided in, no comfort received, and the longing, the all-embracing longing to not be where I was and for this terrible time which just had to be endured, to pass.

Eventually, I learned that I could put myself to sleep anytime, day or night, as a way of escaping and passing through life, obliterating time and avoiding interacting with my father, who – on a practical level – took care of us during my mother's absences. He'd cook simple meals and clean up whilst complaining about my mother's poor housekeeping standards, so sleeping meant that I could avoid listening to him, avoid my anger and pain, and withdraw into sleep's blessed and welcome oblivion. In the absence of appropriate care, children find other ways to soothe their pain. But, this way of coping with feelings just manages by avoiding them – they are not worked through. Healthy ways of coping are not learned because there is no one there to guide you, to help you to feel safe about sharing your feelings. There is no one to accept those feelings, to comfort and console, no one to tell you it will all be OK in the morning, because it won't – or maybe only for a little while. Then – even if they did say this – you would stop believing them because you learn that the good times are always followed by volcanic eruptions, fear and breakages to bodies, minds and – as it happened – our home.

So, any good times become half-decent times at best, and gradually they become impossible to enjoy at all because you know – because it is the way it always is – that, as surely as night follows day, things are going to fall apart. And then, you realise they are getting worse and worse, so that you cannot enjoy any time at all, you cannot trust anyone, and the backdrop to any day is the fear and expectation of violence, disruption of family, home and school – moving away, moving back, away and back again, like a ping-pong ball being batted about and then falling off the table.

5

For me, it was not possible to be confident that my mother would be safe if I slept as a child. I learned this lesson early because one morning I woke to find her sitting on the bed next to me. Her feet were bandaged. During the night, she had fled the house to avoid my father's attack. He chased her, throwing milk bottles at her. Her bare feet were badly cut and she was treated in casualty. Not surprisingly, I began having nightmares about Dad being poisonous and attacking Mum and me trying to protect her. I still loved my father and felt very guilty about these dreams. I would consider running out of school at lunch time to check on him, to make sure my dreams hadn't hurt him.

At night-times, I used to settle into bed and imagine that I was secretly powerful. I imagined that I had a secret life, a secret fort and lots of cavalry. I would imagine arriving triumphantly outside our house, sitting up high and very tall on horseback ahead of, and in charge of, the cavalry behind me. We would take my family, except Dad, away to the safety of the fort. No one would know the location of the fort, which was heavily guarded, secure and had lookouts including me, but – even so – I would still fear his, my dad's, arrival. I grew increasingly resentful and tired of my father's behaviour and longed for the peaceful, normal life my friends enjoyed.

Violence was not the only abuse; it was emotional too. I could not understand why my mum could not wear make-up, why our clothes had to be long and plain and why he destroyed clothes we were given of which he did not approve. I could not understand why he only gave my mum a small fraction of his earnings to provide for us all, including him. And, no, he wasn't saving for a rainy day! Sometimes he wouldn't arrive home at all after pay day – he'd just take off somewhere for the weekend, leaving us without money for food, coal or anything. My mother would have to take us all to the local benefits office to beg for some cash. I recall one of these desperate times, when a worker gave my mum ten shillings out of his own pocket for us – the kindness of strangers.

And, why, I always wondered, did he question Mum about her movements, where she'd been, what she'd been doing. Why didn't he want visitors; why did he say Mum was no good when she worked so hard to look after us? (Even when she had six children, she would go out of an evening to a cleaning job to supplement the pittance he gave her.) Why did he hit my big brother and why did he hit my mum when she tried to protect him? These things affected our everyday life, they were our everyday life, but never acceptable.

There wasn't a fort – or, in reality, a refuge – at that time in the city where I lived. But there was a home for destitute women and children… yes that's what it was called… the Home for Destitute Women and Their Children. No shame intended by its title, I am sure, and thank goodness it existed. My father's violence was often unpredictable, but there were times when we could predict it and my mother would call the NSPCC officer who would arrive in his little red car and take us to the home for destitute women. Or the social worker would take us, or a taxi would be sent for us. Mum would spread a blanket out on the floor and we'd rush round collecting what clothes we could in a desperate effort to leave before he arrived back. Knot the blanket and off we'd go.

Of course, he'd follow and would bang on the door, yelling to be let in. I recall hiding with my mother, fearful and with thumping heart, peeking from behind upstairs windows, trying not to be seen, but desperate to keep him in view. I had to stay close so that, if he got in, I could help to protect my mother, scared he would kill her.

He'd promise to be nice in future. He'd promise all sorts of things. He was more than the abuse to my mother. He could also be warm and lovable. She longed for a normal family life and thought that, if she tried harder, it would all be OK. You see, he blamed her for it all.

So, most of those times, my mother would take us back home to that dark house and I'd settle back into my lovely school. Despite my mother's entreaties – because she felt so ashamed – not to tell anyone what had happened to us, there were occasions when I would feel the need to tell a friend why I'd suddenly disappeared and reappeared. And then I'd feel guilty for letting my mum down. It was never OK – the same repetitive pattern of peace for a while, followed by volcanic eruptions and terror, and then off we'd go – back to the home for destitute women.

Social workers would visit and I'd wait outside, desperately hoping they'd sort it all out, but they didn't. The police would attend when called out, and were firm with my father. They ignored his excuses and protestations that our mum charged him for sex and that she'd hit him. They knew him. They'd take him away, telling my mum to get a good night's sleep. I'd watch out for him arriving home the next day, wondering what sort of mood he'd be in, and what might happen next. I'd go in and let Mum know he was on his way home, and then we'd wait.

6

Don't ever underestimate the difference a uniformed officer, or preferably two or more, can make in a child's life. It was always a relief when the police arrived and I could expect that my mum would be safe for a while. The police were so concerned they sent a senior officer round to tell my dad to mend his ways. This made no difference to him. One day, whilst I was visiting an aunt, I was told that mum had collapsed and been hospitalised. I didn't understand what had happened and instinctively felt frightened and, once again, distraught. Later on, my older brother arrived home from play. 'Dad', he said, 'the kids in the street are saying Mum's in hospital because you hit her again'. I froze, amazed at my brother's courage or stupidity, and held my breath. Dad denied this was the case, and told my brother to ignore the other kids. He was right; he'd not hit Mum on this occasion, but he had hit my brother. Years later, I learned that this incident led my mother to attempt suicide; she was so desperately unhappy and this was why she was in hospital – I nearly lost my mother permanently.

The psychiatrist who interviewed my parents told my father to help Mum more and advised against any further children from then on, four being enough in his opinion and all my mum could cope with. But a fifth, and then a sixth child, was born – my father would not use contraception, though he finally allowed a washing machine. Small steps forward can misleadingly indicate positive change and hopefulness for the future.

One night, when I was about ten years old, I was allowed to stay up late to keep my mother company, probably in the hope that my presence might encourage my father to control himself. Actually, he was entirely capable of controlling himself – after all, had he assaulted anyone outside my family half as frequently as he assaulted my mother, he would have been sent to prison for a *very* long time. My father was late home. My mother and I stood out in the street and saw him in the distance, making his way home, swaying as he did so. We decided to walk up the pathway that skirted the back of our terrace of houses, and from which we had a good view of the back of our house and the entrance which we all used. We watched as my father entered the house, and I looked on, in horror and amazement, as he systematically trashed the downstairs part of our home, sweeping items off shelves and smashing things as he went along.

My mother and I ran to the phone box and called the police. As we waited for the police to arrive, two men walked by on their way home. Concerned, they stopped and asked if we needed help. My mother explained what was happening. The men realised that she was talking about the same person whose company they had enjoyed that evening. They were shocked that such a pleasant, quiet man – 'We would never have believed it' – could be the same one smashing up our home. I, in turn, was shocked by the men's response – how could they not know? How could he, my father be so different that they could not know, nor have any idea what he was like?

The next morning, my father looked at the mess, and so did I. From this mess, he pulled a necklace he'd recently given to me, pleased it had survived. He held it out to me and, although I felt a terrible revulsion and did not want it, I was now too afraid to do anything other than to reach out and take the necklace from him. I never wore it again. In the middle of the mess and chaos stood a clothes airer full of our children's clothes, and his, all washed and ironed by our mum. He had chosen not to trash this; you see he had some self-control.

I changed. I started to feel angry. When my father told my mother scornfully that he didn't need to bother about her because, when he was old, I would look after him, I decided this was a big mistake for him to assume. I decided that my future would not be decided by him; this would not be how I would end up. I was deeply unhappy and increasingly determined not to keep on along the terrible repetitive path of abuse, family separations, being reunited, abuse, separations and so on. This had all become entirely predictable, and hope of change ebbed away with the experience of repeated disappointment, fear and violence.

I asked my mum to take us away or – if we were away – to stay away and not return to my father. I did not realise how difficult this would be for her, without somewhere suitable to live, and lonely for her without our dad, not to mention caring for all us kids. And, he was of course violent to her whether she lived with him or not. However, although I was angry and fed up, my younger brothers and sister had not reached that point and wanted to be with their dad. Most importantly, there was no one to help my mum to understand or to support her with the many complex feelings, including those of loss and grief, that make many women in her circumstance yearn for their partners, remaining hopeful of positive change even though they continue to be abusive.

7

One day my dad arrived to collect us all from the home for destitute women, my mother having decided to return home. I, however, decided that I was not going to go back home and ran away, walking miles across the city and asked to be taken into care. I was listened to and placed in a residential children's home. This meant a change of junior school. After several more episodes of bouncing between home, the home for destitute women and the children's home, it was from the latter that I made my way across the city for my first terrifying day at secondary school, where, yet again, I would meet up with old friends from junior school whom I had not seen for a long period. I don't recall them asking any questions, just accepting me back and, after my initial awkwardness, I enjoyed the continuity of their friendship. And so it went on.

When I was away from home, I would become terribly homesick for my mum and siblings and, despite my reluctance, would eventually move back there. Of course, the same old pattern repeated itself, and we'd find ourselves back in the home for destitute women. I'd refuse to return home and would move back into the children's home. And, each time this happened, I grew stronger, more determined and gradually able to stay away from home for longer periods. Sometimes, my parents would both arrive at the children's home and try to get me to return home with them; my response was sometimes to run away. One night, I walked around until very late, scared of the dark and dodging behind garden hedges to hide, if any traffic appeared – I remembered to take care of myself in relation to avoiding the attention of strangers, my mother having, ironically, always warned us about stranger danger. Tired and wanting to sleep I crept into some stranger's back garden, borrowed a small rug from their garden shed, put it over a stone to make a pillow and there I slept. Early next morning, I returned the rug to its rightful place and then returned to the children's home.

It was on one of the occasions that I returned home, when I was 11 years old, that things were to change dramatically. This is where I must return to the incident mentioned earlier when I was angry with my father about his complaints regarding an evening meal which had been kept warm for him and by the time he arrived home was a little dry. I responded to his comments, explaining that earlier when he'd been expected home, the meal had been lovely. I turned and walked away from him, returning to the kitchen where my mother was. Suddenly I was pushed outside through the door by my mum and told to run. Next thing, she had hold of me and I found myself being rushed to the phone box to call an ambulance and the police. In her hand and dripping with blood was the kitchen knife. A younger brother came hopping down the road towards us with only one shoe on – I wondered if he'd hurt himself on the knife. Then, I heard my mother telling the emergency services that she'd hit my father in the neck with the knife.

Unbeknown to me, my father had followed me to the kitchen. My mother had looked up from what she was doing and realised he was going to attack me, probably for what I had said to him. He had immediately dropped unconscious. He needed three stitches and was home the next day. Neighbours gathered round my mother as we sat in the police car watching my father being placed in the ambulance; the neighbours said they hoped he was dead and that, at last, he'd gotten what he deserved. My mother had no such thought – she was totally distraught at what she'd done. No doubt my father went down in official records as a battered husband.

We were taken to the police station and separated from our mother. A female police officer passed a message to me that I should look after the younger children. No longer numb with shock and confusion, my body was now bent double, racked with pain and tears. Our mother who had endured years of abuse and had sought to protect me was taken from us and placed on remand in Risley prison. I visited her there once, but was so overwhelmed by the place I could hardly speak. She was later placed on probation and moved to a women's hostel. We children were initially placed in a children's home familiar to me and large enough to have space for us all. To have been separated from brothers and sister at this time would have been beyond endurance.

Finally, my mother was given effective help – support – rehousing. And custody was to be decided through the courts. I began having nightmares in the form of a long empty court corridor which I would have to walk along alone. At the end of the corridor, I would have to decide whether to turn right or left; one way led to my mother and the other way to my father, but I didn't know which way led to whom. Imagine my anxiety as I approached the end of the corridor and the possibility of taking the wrong direction and having to leave the court with my father.

I knew my father to be convincing – what if the real-life court believed him and not my mother – remember the two men who often socialised with him and knew nothing about his behaviour at home! This was a terrifying prospect. Thankfully, the court decided we should remain with our mother.

But, there was another nightmare – a real living one – that went on and on, week after week after week. My father would turn up any time he fancied, and expect to be provided with a meal. Frequently he would arrive late at night, thumping on the door, yelling abuse and demanding to be let in. If I had gone to sleep, I would be woken, and, still afraid that my father would murder my mother, I was terrified. Mum had to stay with the younger children, so I would have to sneak out of the house and, in the dark and late at night, run up a – usually – quiet lane, across a busy road and onto the nearby housing estate to a public phone box to call the police, begging them to come as quickly as possible. One night I had to do this three times – it was a different station now that we'd moved to another part of the city.

'Hurry, please hurry', I'd beg and yell down the phone telling them what was happening and 'He's trying to get in, he's trying to get in!' The police arrived... 'He's gone' they said, but I knew he hadn't, I knew him.

Desperately scanning the area, my eyes found him, hiding behind a lamp post. Now the police saw him off.

One of my younger brothers hadn't reached the stage of being completely fed up with our father and desperately wanted to have contact with him. Dad was not reliable, sometimes turning up for contact and sometimes not. He also sent messages that, if Mum didn't have him back, he would not see my brother again. Painful for my brother, and also for my mother, to see him in such pain. You see, each child in a family will have their individual feelings and needs according to their experiences.

8

And then suddenly you are an adult faced with normal conflict in relationships and what happens? You withdraw, because it takes longer to work out what it is you are feeling, and you don't want to be like your parents, screaming and throwing things around or beating the living daylights out of someone. But at the same time you don't have the skills or confidence to communicate calmly and assertively. And your parents have role-modelled the understanding that conflict cannot be worked through – it has to be either avoided or 'resolved' through controlling, humiliating and brutalising someone to get your own way. Ultimately, you have learned that it leads to separation, repeatedly, so you get stuck with both wanting to leave and trying to avoid this, and with trying to make sense of everything, continually analysing the past for clues about why you feel this way now, and wanting to behave differently. And, it is really hard to ask for help, because you get reminded constantly by your memories about all that shame that you felt as a child about what happened in your home, about your dad beating your mum up, what the neighbours heard, what your friends thought about you, about having to suddenly leave the area and your school, not being able to tell anyone why, and then arriving back as suddenly as you left and not knowing what to say to the other kids who have been getting on with their – apparently – steady, comfortable lives, as per normal. You also know your mum and dad have told you not to say anything about why you left suddenly – what a burden – and, of course, the guilt and fear you felt, at the time, in case your mum and dad found out that – despite it all – you did not manage to keep the information in and just had to tell a friend where you'd been and why you'd been away.

Somewhere along the line, because you got so used to keeping all those feelings inside, you learned that you had to be emotionally self-sufficient, and, you carried this knowledge into adulthood so that, by the time you becamse an adult, telling someone about what happened or asking for help becomes too difficult. You might need some help figuring it out, so it doesn't mess up your adult life and then your kids' lives, but the old feelings of shame and fear of how you will be judged by others start jumping up and down inside, and reminding you that you don't want to feel weak and afraid all over again. So you carry on trying to manage all by yourself – well, it seems endless and feels exhausting.

9

My parents had a couple of further brief reconciliations, as I grew up. One of these was when I was 18 years old. By now, I had started to think that my parents would still be trying to work things out between them into their 80s. Me, I had my eyes on the future. I had decided to work hard at school, obtain qualifications and work towards achieving a career so that if I got married, had children and it all went wrong I would not be trapped and financially dependent, but able to work and provide a safe, well-resourced home for my children. No one was going to be able to tell me – as one benefits officer told my mother when she asked for some help with funding to provide a much-needed holiday for us – 'People like you can't expect to go away on holiday'. I will never forget the hurt on my mother's face.

When I was 18 years old and my parents decided to reunite, I allowed myself to consider the possibility that perhaps, over the years, my father might have changed. Together with my mother, I visited him. I reasoned with myself that, if instead of making excuses, he could now take responsibility for his behaviour, then I would know he'd changed for the better and could feel some optimism for the future and... wouldn't it be lovely to at last have a mum *and* a proper dad?

Well, he denied and played down his violence, also blaming my mum for any problems in the past, so I knew this would not work out. Later, I asked my mum for time to leave home before he moved in. Soon after, and probably angry that I wasn't welcoming him back with open arms and wishing to assert himself, my father towered over me, yelling that I was 'nothing, a no one, been nowhere, going nowhere, you are nothing!' He was as wrong about that as he'd been about the choices he'd made in relation to his behaviour over the past many years. I left home that day to live with friends, before moving into my own rented accommodation. I vowed never to return home again, but to build my own life. I decided that I would not allow my father to damage my adult life as he had my childhood. I had had no choice then, but now I did.

My parents' reconciliation lasted three weeks.

I never saw my father again.

I have no regrets about that decision.

10

It was a hard and lengthy journey from that point to where I am now. But it is not surprising that the journey to recovery, for me and for other adults in the same situation, is a long road. After all, when the two most important people in your early life – your mum and dad – whom you would most naturally expect to be able to consistently love you and be by your side – are unable to do so, it is bound to be deeply damaging for children. This happens often when one is abusive (and we need to be extremely clear that being a domestic abuser is abusive and neglectful of children – it is most definitely poor parenting practice) and the other parent has to be so mindful of keeping herself and her children safe, which can involve repeated separations from them – not only physical ones, but also emotional ones – that, no matter how hard she tries to avoid it, her energy for parenting and meeting the children's needs is focused elsewhere, undermined and diminished. The sense of abandonment that children may have in these circumstances, their loss of childhood spontaneity and confidence that all will be well, and their knowing far too early in life the harsher and crueller aspects of human nature – the impact of these experiences that, over time and repetition, become part of our deepest core experiences, should not be underestimated in terms of their potential for long-standing harm.

11

Many years later, I attended a trade union conference held to raise awareness about the extent and impact of domestic abuse. I was in the audience and found myself reflecting on my own experiences and journey. The very salutary thought crossed my mind that I was in my mid-thirties, and felt as though I was only just beginning to feel some real sense of self-worth, of possibly being lovable. The second thought was that it had taken too long to achieve this sense of inner self, too long to recover from what had happened so long ago, and I did not want it to take this long for anyone else.

For myself, at that point, I recognised the need to do something to promote change. I did not want it to take so long for others to recover from childhood domestic abuse. So I began to study. The first book I read was written by Gill Hague and Ellen Malos: *Domestic Violence: Action for Change* (first edition, 1993). At last, a framework for understanding that made sense and – like jigsaw pieces coming together inside me for the first time – I recognised myself and my experiences not only as being deeply understood, but also as finally acknowledged and openly identified by someone else. For the first time, I felt understood. For the first time, I felt my own effort to understand my father's and mother's behaviour was acknowledged and immeasurably enhanced. I felt relieved, strong, a survivor.

The journey from that time to this has been remarkable, and it is difficult to describe in summary. I achieved a professional career, one of which I believe that my old headmaster and social worker would be proud. I have not had to use my career earnings to provide alternative accommodation for myself and my – now grown up – son. My husband and I have been together for over 30 years. There have been many challenges along the way, and I have had to grow the confidence to love without holding back just in case the most important people in my adult life let me down like my dad had done. I have learned that I can rely on others to help me – I do not have to be totally self-sufficient, that I can love and am lovable, that I have the strength to cope with adversity, that the shame of my childhood was not mine to carry, and that imagination is not just about surviving.

Imagination is – in my view – the well-spring of our humanity, and carries with it the capacity for being reunited with playfulness, and healing. Yes, you may correctly assume that I have been helped along my way by therapy, the nurturing and growth of self-awareness provided in that space.

Earlier, I stated that I have no regrets about my decision to walk away from my father. I do, however, regret that the little girl, now grown up and with a loving family of her own, and who now writes this chapter for Gill Hague's gift of a book to us all, was not able to keep the father she loved so much. I regret that the help was not available to adequately challenge and support my father to change and grow a life for his family based on respect, decency and love.

I regret that services were not available to help my father when he was a child to recover from his own painful experience of childhood domestic abuse. My father's life as a child, and as an adult, was not a happy one. His attempts to cope with his pain through control and violence led to an unhappy life for himself, as well as for others, and estrangement from those he loved, but sought to control. He wrongly anticipated that his child would continue to give him the sort of unconditional love and acceptance that he was unable to provide for her.

I regret that the words my mother asked me to pass on to others when I became an activist are still needed today. She asked me to tell whoever would listen to:

- tell a woman she can survive and come through

- help her cope with the loneliness

- tell her it is not her fault.

Most of all, I regret that, although there has been huge growth in the recognition and understanding of domestic abuse, affected children can still not take for granted that effective action will be taken by relevant agencies to protect them, to require and support positive change in their families, and to provide them with therapeutic services to support their recovery from the trauma of domestic abuse. I hope that this book can help in the long process of change for children of the future.

Chapter 6

Dealing with it at the Time

*Working with Children Exposed
to Domestic Violence to Enable
Less Painful Later Adulthoods*

The focus of this book is on adults who experienced childhood domestic violence, and practice interventions with adults are discussed in detail in Chapter 8. Thus, the book is not designed to be a detailed text about work with children. However, interventions with children experiencing domestic abuse may well be of help in terms of the adults they become. Thus, in this chapter, we briefly discuss ways of working with children exposed to domestic violence specifically to enable them to move forward to less painful adulthoods. What can we do to intercept the difficulties discussed in previous chapters before the person concerned has grown up?

The chapter concentrates specifically on direct work with children with a long-term aim. It is not about work with abused or neglected children as a whole, but specifically about recovering from experiences of maltreatment and domestic violence. Thus, what it is not about is child protection work, assessment procedures, safeguarding arrangements, childcare legislation or legal proceedings. Nor is it about handling disclosures of domestic violence, social work case planning and interventions, or safety planning with children to ensure personal safety in conditions of domestic abuse. Discussions about these various issues already exist in abundance in the literature. Those requiring a practitioner handbook on direct children's work, child protection and domestic violence will need to look elsewhere, but may find the references in the book of help.

Of course, all of the above issues regarding social work and child protection interventions will have impacts on outcomes for children when they become adults in regard, for example, to the sensitivity and effectiveness of any child protection work conducted with them and whether they were able to be adequately safeguarded and to leave behind the violence. However, recovery work with children and young people who have experienced domestic abuse tends to be a wider-ranging project than the type of interventions provided by children's and family social services departments.

A 2006 paper tracing the development of social care practice in relation to child witnesses of domestic violence, for example, found that this work tended to be overtaken by child protection processes (Rivett and Kelly 2006). While the resulting legal and policy initiatives had quite often failed, the needs of the children were frequently subsumed under them. The paper concludes that children experiencing domestic abuse should not always be assumed only to need bureaucratic child protection responses, but rather there should be a wider understanding of their needs and the provision of creative and responsive services. Within this provision, it is vital to incorporate their own views and voices.

If children have strong attachments with a non-abusing parent and/ or are able to escape from situations of domestic abuse, perhaps with the intervention of a refuge, and move on to lead happier new lives, this can help hugely. Alternatively, those whose families stay together may be able to develop safety strategies and context-specific ways of coping, and then move satisfactorily towards adulthood, especially where a close relationship exists with the mother/main caregiver (Mullender *et al.* 2002). Either way, safety and a loving environment will assist in good outcomes.

Thus, effective social interventions which enable such outcomes are required, as are sufficient domestic violence support services, including child support provision. Assuming such an ensured provision of services, and it is a big assumption in the 2011 context of cuts in public spending, this chapter concentrates on how to assist beneficial long-term outcomes. It presents some ideas for work with children to enable healing and a move for them towards a contented, balanced future (in a way which was not available to the adults who have contributed testimonies and poems to this book). As an overview, the chapter includes brief sections on resilience, children's services in refuges, individual counselling, one-to-one support work and group work, with some coverage of specific techniques for healing and growing.

Some overall issues

In general, the literature has demonstrated that children can recover from detrimental experiences of domestic violence. Studies conducted so far on how to work with children have been reviewed in the UK by Hester *et al.* (2007). Drawing on this review and on others, issues to be taken into account by professionals can be considered to include:

- providing both protection and support for child victims

- listening to, and taking on board, children's views

- working with the non-abusive parent

- helping mothers to be safe

- attempting to avoid overly punitive responses

- attempting, similarly, to avoid 'knee-jerk', overly procedural responses – these are extremely complex and sensitive issues

- avoiding mother-blaming or victim-blaming responses, while protecting the children involved

- developing/providing safe accommodation, refuge, focused counselling, and advocacy, support networks, outreach and group work with affected children

- working on the issue in a multi-agency context in partnership between statutory and voluntary third-sector services

- participating in established multi-agency initiatives (for example domestic abuse forums)

- developing domestic violence training for all relevant professionals, including on the impacts on children, and agreeing specific domestic violence policies.

The first priority for engaging in work of this type with children is ensuring safety. Children can recover most successfully if it is possible for the violence to be eliminated from their lives (Hester *et al.* 2007; Mullender *et al.* 2002; Rossman 1998), and the safety of the mother or non-abusing parent will affect outcomes for the child. Thus, the primary and underlying issues for policy-makers and practitioners are that effective intervention involves at best the following: the elimination, where possible, of the violence, personal safety, recovery work, even if limited to 'talking about it', support strategies to enable positivity and empowerment, and the building in of protective factors (Hester *et al.* 2007), as discussed in the later section of this chapter on 'Resilience'.

It has been known for many years that moving to a situation of non-violence and being surrounded by loving family (or other) support are likely to lead to the best outcomes as adults. However, while a cessation of domestic abuse is helpful, it cannot always be achieved. Further, just moving away from the violence may not be sufficient (see for example Peled 1997). Rather, ongoing emotional support, nurturing and possibly professional therapeutic assistance are likely to be needed in some situations. Where such nurturing support is provided by practitioners in the field, they need to understand the dynamics of domestic abuse and to adopt an empowering response, as further discussed below. Validation of the child and their experiences is key. So also is enabling them to be able to differentiate between violent conflict and non-violent disagreement, and to build strategies into their lives, both as children and as adults, to deal with conflict resolution and experiences of violence (see for example Rivett, Howarth and Harold 2006). One of the key ways to start to do this is to be on the child's side in a broad sense, to listen, and to be reliable in responding appropriately.

Unfortunately, this does not always happen. Practitioners, in the past at least, have often let children down badly (Mullender *et al.* 2002). Now that the impacts of domestic abuse on children are recognised and services have been developed, however, there is the opportunity for professionals to respond more effectively. They need to recognise that the damage done to children and young people may be such that ongoing emotional support may be needed. Children's confidence, self-esteem and internal 'feeling' of having a place in the world may be deeply eroded. But, often for the very same children, their ability to cope, or at least to keep going while sometimes carrying debilitating emotional scars, is remarkable and in some cases heroic. Those attempting to assist, and to improve on, previously poor or badly informed responses need to start right there.

The first issue: children's work in domestic violence services and Women's Aid

To begin with, in moving now to look at specific ways of working with children and at practice responses, the importance of children's services provided by domestic violence organisations must again be highlighted. These are the only specialist services and the main providers of support for children affected by domestic violence. They have been developed over many years by the Women's Aid federations, the Refuge organisation and other refuges and domestic violence support services, and include interactive resources like the Hideout website and children's *Message Board*, briefly described in Chapter 2 and considered in more detail in the section on 'Children's participation' below. Over the years since their foundation in the 1970s, children's domestic violence services have developed innovative practice and expertise, often without adequate or sustained funding (Hester *et al*. 2007), as we have discussed throughout.

Children's workers usually offer a combination of group work, individual one-to-one work, advocacy and practical support (see Hague *et al*. 2000; Hester *et al*. 2007; Humphreys *et al*. 2000). Studies of children's workers in refuge organisations (see Hague *et al*. 1996; Hague *et al*. 2000) have identified the creative and imaginative work with children that is often conducted, with workers 'getting alongside' children in a way not often seen in other social service organisations. Such work may include sessions in a dedicated play room, and informal (or formal) 'key-working' and counselling about the abuse experiences. Children's workers also provide parenting support, outdoor activities, trips and holidays away, holiday play schemes, play sessions, advocacy on behalf of children, and mentoring and liaison with schools, with youth schemes, and with children and family social services. Some are committed to the direct decision-making participation of children to plan and manage the activities provided.

Children often benefit from being able to express themselves, both in general, and to talk about the abuse with children's workers in domestic violence services, and this can be through art and play, as well as verbally. They also may need to deal with feelings of rage and anger and with confusing emotions of love for the perpetrator (often their father) and recognised or unrecognised grief. Some children have related behavioural problems which children's workers may be able to address. Third-sector domestic violence services are able to take on such issues, often in creative ways, and may have many years of experience that statutory workers may lack (Community Care 2011; Hague *et al*. 2000). The contribution of children's workers in refuges and domestic violence services to recovery in adulthood for the children and young people with whom they work cannot be over-emphasised.

However, as we alluded to in Chapter 2, a 2011 Women's Aid survey found that domestic and sexual violence services in the UK, including children's workers and projects, were being cut so much under government cutbacks – in some areas by nearly 100 per cent – that as many as 70,000 abused women and children could be left without support in 2012 (Community Care 2011; Women's Aid 2011a). Nearly two-thirds of refuge services had no council funding at all at the time of the survey. However, without the continued and improved provision of such third-sector and social work services (including refuges, children's services within them, and specialist provision for black and minority communities), we will be failing children experiencing domestic violence in the future.

Just listening and offering a helping hand

This section is about listening. We begin, therefore, by listening to the informants for this book, before expanding the discussion to the wider literature. We build on the words of the adult survivors of childhood domestic violence in the interviews and testimonies within the book in terms of what they believed would have helped as children. The testimony-givers and the focus group participants ranged in age from their 20s to their 60s. Thus, their views about services were from some years ago. Noting this, our respondents pointed out that better support services are still needed, together with child-friendly approaches which are sympathetic, understanding and culturally aware. Within this, they particularly highlighted the need to maintain and resource refuges – and children's services within them – as a vital source of support for vulnerable children exposed to domestic violence.

In the focus group, all the members pointed out that things have improved greatly in the last two decades in terms of domestic violence and its impacts on children being taken seriously. However, only two had had any access to services themselves. These contacts had been moderately useful, often in terms of an individual worker who took the time to help. Only one focus group participant had been in a refuge, which had been a mixed experience but broadly beneficial, especially in terms of input from the children's and refuge workers, who had listened, been supportive and made her feel important. Both 'Rose Wood' and 'Anna' who contributed testimonies had stayed in refuges and the experience had been useful and had saved them from abuse during the time there were there.

Along with participants emphasising the need for more refuge and other domestic violence services, almost all of them, especially those who had not used any services, identified what would have helped the most was for 'it not to have happened' (focus group member). Overall in terms of overcoming the impacts, listening and having someone to talk with were major issues for all of our informants, confirming the findings of various previous research studies (see for example Hester *et al.* 2007; McGee 2000; Mullender *et al.* 2002; Radford and Hester 2006). Indeed, in the Mullender *et al.* study, detailed in the book, *Children's Perspectives on Domestic Violence*, and in the partner book in children's own words, *Stop Hitting Mum!* (Mullender *et al.* 2002 and 2003), one of the main findings was how much children wished to be consulted, involved and talked with about the domestic abuse they were experiencing, and possible solutions. In that study, though, almost none of the practitioners had asked them about it – ever.

Children are, however, social actors and active agents in their own lives (Mullender *et al.* 2002). Most of the relevant literature confirms this finding: that their voices need to be heard (where this can be achieved safely) and that they need to be believed, validated and supported, if practitioners are to help with the recovery process. Giving children the time to reflect on their lives, not rushing them, facilitating expression of anger and distress, validating their experiences, their fears and their feelings, listening to them, supporting them and believing in them (not just believing them) are the key issues (Hester *et al.* 2007; Jaffe *et al.* 1990; Mullender *et al.* 2002).

Diversity in responses and communicating appropriately

For practitioners, an important issue is to communicate with the child in an age-appropriate way and at a level that they can manage and understand. There are particular techniques for communicating in different ways with children, including the very young, and training course are available in so doing. The Thomas Coram Institute, for example, runs courses on appropriate communication skills with toddlers and pre-school children. Similarly, the Institute for Arts in Therapy and Education (London) offers a varied range of courses for practitioners interested in developing skills in the use of expressive arts to promote children's development throughout the age range. In a third example, the Tavistock Centre (The Tavistock and Portman NHS Foundation Trust in London) offers relevant courses in therapeutic communication with children from a psychodynamic perspective.

Communication is bigger than talking and may include the use of play, creative materials and expressive art. For children with communication or other impairments or who are part of the Deaf community,[1] effective communication techniques have been developed, and practitioners need to explore the resources, training and advice available about such issues if

---

1   Many members of the Deaf community prefer for the word 'Deaf' to be capitalised and this practice is followed throughout this book.

they are not themselves familiar with the work or do not have the requisite skills.

All work with children who have had experiences of domestic violence needs to go at the child's own pace so that they are not – and/or do not feel – coerced into 'treatment', which might then to some extent mirror the way that they might have been forced into difficult home situations. Therapeutic play, the use of story, visualisation, drama, puppets, toys, tools, art and video can be of help, as discussed throughout this chapter. Importantly, diversity issues are key. Silvern *et al.* (1995), for instance, demonstrated that individual therapeutic work needs to take on ethnicity and class, economic status, family structures, and other issues of equality, in a sensitive and well-informed way, and many subsequent studies confirm and develop these findings (Imam and Akhtar 2005; Mullender *et al.* 2002).

It is important, for example, to understand the complexities of the issues for minority communities. Young people of South Asian origin, interviewed for the Mullender *et al.* (2002) study of children's perspectives on domestic violence, spoke of having to be careful and strategic in dealing with practitioners and social workers who might misunderstand cultural issues and respond inappropriately (Imam and Akhtar 2005). Most of these children in the study also expressed fears of racism and racial abuse. Further, they explained how social work interventions might focus on encouraging women and children to leave home due to domestic abuse, which, for them, would have removed their wider patterns of support in the extended family and might not always work well in South Asian contexts (although a large network of specialist South Asian refuges does exist). The young South Asian children interviewed suggested that alternative strategies needed to be considered and developed.

Further issues involved in one-to-one work with children are discussed in more detail below. Overall, domestic violence is, of course, a very difficult subject to raise with children. Some practitioners shy away from it due to awkwardness, fear or embarrassment, or may decide it is just not worth taking the risk. However, it should be borne in mind that if social workers and other practitioners are able to key into children's experiences and to be in tune with the child on this issue, the outcomes could be transformative. The most important thing may be, therefore, to not turn away.

Children's participation, *Listen Louder* and hearing their voices

Listening to children is now enshrined in the historic UN Convention on the Rights of the Child (UN 1989). The UK, however, in common with many other countries, fails to meet its obligations under this Convention every time it is assessed (Merrick 2006). For example, a recent review by a coalition of children's rights organisations, coordinated through the Children's Rights Alliance for England and entitled *For the Incorporation of the United Nations Convention on the Rights of the Child into UK Law 2010* (Rights of the Child UK (ROCK) 2011), includes wide-ranging critiques of the UK Government's response. Nevertheless, children's participation in policy-making and in agency operation, as well as their right to be heard on all issues that affect them personally is now widely accepted. CAFCASS, the NSPCC and other child care organisations all operate children's participation and consultation schemes.

The Women's Aid federations have conducted many consultations with children and young people about domestic violence. Women's Aid in England has run a variety of direct consultation programmes, for example *Kidspeak* in which young people were directly consulted about their views. Refuge organisations also commonly consult the children living there about issues which affect them. The second author of this book has experience of being invited into a local refuge to review the child service provision with the resident children. The children were directly consulted and actively participated, expressing their views clearly and cogently. (Their experiences of living in the refuge were largely positive with the exception that they would have liked more play support to be available during the evenings.)

Scottish Women's Aid ran a *Listen Louder Campaign* from 2001 until 2004 in which children were widely consulted. *Listen Louder* involved large numbers of children experiencing domestic violence who participated through a variety of routes. These included high-profile annual meetings with ministers and politicians, the participation of children in new research studies, and the production of DVDs and other publicity materials. The engagement of children and young people at the highest level politically in Scotland was an especially effective (and unusual) feature of the programme (Houghton 2006). Thus, the campaign aimed to give them a voice and to encourage government and others to listen to what they were saying. As a result, Scottish Women's Aid and *Listen Louder* submitted a petition to the Scottish Parliament asking for service gaps identified by the children and young people to be addressed and minimum standards ensured. They published newsletters written by young people and developed multimedia presentations including an exhibition of artwork, writing and films. They also ran a 'textathon' with young people texting and emailing their support, and put on events for practitioners and policy-makers run by children. The campaign resulted in a £6 million award from the Scottish Government to improve services for children and young people across Scotland (Scottish Women's Aid 2011).

Participation in this way can give rise to feeling needed, respected and listened to. Being part of something 'bigger', making a difference and assisting other children exposed to domestic abuse can assist children and young people to overcome their own negative or difficult experiences. As discussed in Chapter 4, listening to both adults and children, and raising their voices, can help to build confidence and a widespread understanding that living in a family where there is domestic violence is not something to be ashamed of as a child, and not his or her fault. A child may often think that they are the only one having such experiences, and joining with others can be empowering, especially where there is a positive outcome, as for *Listen Louder*.

The Hideout website, specifically for children and young people experiencing domestic violence, also helps to build confidence around the issue, presents alternatives and is interactive (Hideout 2011). For example, the site provides an interactive *Message Board* to facilitate children 'having their say' which is widely used for both children and young people to exchange views and ideas. The *Message Board*, an extremely popular innovation, enables them to gain information and contacts, and often to feel that they are not alone and can also wield some influence. The Hideout hosts live chats with experts, Twitter feeds, interactive sharing of personal stories and direct consultations on issues that have an impact on children and young people. By using such approaches and routes, children can feel empowered, better able to deal with the domestic abuse in their lives, and perhaps able to grow up into a less scarred adulthood.

Resilience, coping and protective factors

It is not rocket science to be able to understand that being listened to, participating in solutions, and being taken seriously can all make major contributions to building children's emotional strength. These approaches can enhance their ability to cope, their adaptability in adverse situations and any feelings they may have of positive agency and competence. Such qualities can often contribute to what is known as 'resilience', commonly regarded as a key factor in recovery, as noted throughout this book. There is a considerable literature on resilience in relation to adverse experiences of different types (Grotberg 1995, 1997). Resilience is the idea that people have different capacities that allow them to overcome (or not) the negative effects of trauma or adversity, such as experiencing domestic abuse. 'Protective factors' can help build children's resilience, while 'risk factors' can reduce it (see, for example, Garmezy and Rutter 1983; Hester *et al.* 2007; Kashani and Allen 1998). Successful coping with adverse experiences of any type appears to depend not only on the strength of these protective factors but also on their occurrence in some sort of combination, rather than singly (Jaffe *et al.* 1990; Kashani and Allen 1998).

There is now copious research on resilience in terms of trying to uncover issues that would help children resist stress and trauma (for example Masten 2001). Resilience is thought to develop as the child, often without realising it, draws on techniques which have been successful in coping with stress in the past, and then repeats them. However, what is often obscured is how the individual child actually interprets and understands their own strengths and resilience (Anderson and Danis 2007). Helping children and young people to uncover and recognise both the impacts of the abuse and their personal strategies and strengths for coping or for resisting trauma – and mobilising these – is a good way forward.

In relation to children and young people living with domestic violence, specifically, there is much research evidence confirming the importance of protective factors and coping strategies, as briefly discussed in Chapter 2. The severity of the domestic violence and the length of time that children are exposed to it are important risk factors for children's resilience and for their future adult lives (Edleson 1999; Grych *et al.* 2000), as is the type of abuse experienced. Conversely, general preventative strategies, which are likely to assist both adults and children in coping well with trauma – as opposed to being unable to cope – include the presence of fewer life stressors (on top of the causal trauma itself). Factors and behaviours which contribute to building resilience and helpful coping mechanisms include: positive self-esteem; personality factors (being easy-going and humorous, for instance); secure attachment to non-abusive parents or care-givers; the existence of networks of personal support and of community and social frameworks; being able to escape; having some purchase and agency in the situation; and participating in support activities (see Bancroft and Silverman 2002; Humphreys 2001; Mullender *et al.* 2002; Rutter

1985). Thus, mediating factors which help children and young people cope are complex and numerous, with different factors sometimes being emphasised by different authors.

In more detail, self-esteem emerges as a critical element in successful coping (see, for example, Garmezy 1983; Hester et al. 2007). However, many studies have found that self-esteem is often damaged particularly for children experiencing domestic violence, so that there may be a re-stigmatising or 'doubly negative' effect in terms of coping (Abrahams 1994; Hester et al. 2007; McGee 2000; Mullender et al. 2002). Clearly then, building self-esteem needs to be a key objective for practitioners and those trying to help, including non-abusive parents or care-givers.

Overall, mothers (or mother-substitutes) who are able to parent well and non-violently have been found to be perceived by their children as positively supportive, and are important moderators of the impact of the abuse (Worrall, Boylan and Roberts 2008), as noted throughout this chapter. Almost all research accounts suggest that secure attachment and a warm loving relationship to a non-violent parent or other significant care-giving adult is important. Thus, mothers, in particular, play an important role in children's resilience. Hughes et al. (2001), for example, found that children's resilience may be linked to the mental health of their mothers (see, also, Worrall et al. 2008). In many (although not all) instances of domestic violence, children and mothers may well share strong and supportive relationships with each other which thus may contribute creatively to their ability to get through the experience. This is the case despite the 'minefield' nature of the relationships between some mothers and their children after domestic violence (Mullender et al. 2002).

Other factors that have been found to enhance children's resilience include support provided by their family, friends and community (Mullender et al. 2002) and by having a supportive relationship with another adult or family member (Levondosky, Bogat and von Eye 2000), as noted in Chapter 2. Thus, supportive family and community relations are very helpful but, frequently, in cases of domestic abuse, grandmothers and family members may have been (perhaps temporarily) lost due to having to move away or 'hide' in a refuge, just at the time when, according to the specialist literature on the subject cited above, children may need them most. Overall, then, it can be seen that coping with domestic violence is likely to be additionally traumatic, when compared with other adverse situations where children are less likely to lose their homes, families and communities.

A word of caution is probably advisable in looking at resilience, especially in terms of possible judgemental reactions to those who seem to lack it. Relatively little is known about the factors that determine the extent to which an experience of emotional abuse predicts later psychosocial functioning. Children may seem to cope well at the time, but the impacts may manifest themselves later, triggered by different developmental stages or experiences reminiscent of previous abuse. A wide variety of studies have identified complex factors that may determine risk and later resilience in children which include: a) complex predisposing issues (such as early care-giving experiences); b) precipitating factors (like the frequency, intensity and duration of traumatic experiences); c) individual personality factors intrinsic to the particular child such as how they view themselves and others, internal or external attributions of blame, behavioural patterns, self-worth and general disposition; and d) external factors such as school, friendships and whether they are abusive or bullying or not, and the availability of supportive relationships (see Iwaniec 2006; Iwaniec *et al.* 2006). The experiences of child victims vary widely, as do the protective factors involved, so that prescriptive solutions rarely apply.

Thus, understanding resilience is sometimes more complicated than the literature might seem to suggest. Children may be partly resilient but they may also be partly frightened, shy, mortified by their experiences and caught in cycles of emotional pain, self-blaming and confusion. The existence of such difficulties does not mean that the child does not also have some resilience. In general, testing resilience has proved difficult in terms of building robust research evidence. Little is yet known about why resilience is forged within some adverse situations but not others, or the context-specific forms that it might take, as well as the way in which it can be a changing quality, constantly adapting to the interplay between protective and risk factors (Anderson and Danis 2007). An understanding of diversity is particularly key in analysing this complex picture in regard to resilience, as well as to interventions (as outlined above). Ways of coping and being resilient may vary in different cultural, class, ethnic and religious groupings (Imam and Akhtar 2005).

Resiliency manuals and guides

A variety of resiliency manuals and studies exist, mainly in a North American context, that can be drawn on and that can assist with building personal resilience and emotional strength for children and young people. In the renowned (1997) 'International Resilience Project', for example,

Edith Grotberg has presented a variety of research findings and guides, in key work on resilience across 30 countries. In her text, *A Guide to Promoting Resilience in Children* Grotberg (1995) provided a useful practical guide that can help adults, including both parents and caretakers, to promote resilience in children. For different age groups of children, the *Guide* identified actions by helping adults which might be expected to promote resilience – and, conversely, actions which might be expected to have the opposite effect, and are therefore to be avoided.

The Resilience Research Centre, based in Dalhousie University, Nova Scotia, Canada, brings together scholars and practitioners in the field of resilience research from different disciplines and cultural backgrounds. The Centre works collaboratively with partners in about 20 countries across six continents. One of its programmes, 'Negotiating Resilience' is a visual methods qualitative study on pathways to resilience focusing on how young people from many different countries cope with daily challenges. The study uses visual methods, including film, video, photographs and pictures, to capture a day in the life of each participating young person, who is then directly involved in analysing the data, to attempt to identify 'hidden' aspects of resilience that have previously escaped attention. Many of these dimensions of resilience are culturally embedded. The project suggests that the Western individualistic focus of much work on resilience has overlooked such factors in people's lives across the globe.

Through its own International Resilience Project, the Resilience Research Centre has produced multiple publications on building resilience in young people in different cultural contexts and for a wide variety of types of adversity, often using strengths-based approaches with attention to project evaluation, life story approaches, cultural sensitivity and community development in widely different context (see for example Cameron, Lau and Tapanya 2009; Ungar 2011). These studies shift our understanding of resilience from an individualistic concept, popular with Western-trained researchers and human services providers, to a more culturally embedded understanding of well-being.

Individual one-to-one work with children

In this section, we further expand on the earlier discussion about practice with children, taking account of the above consideration of resilience. Such individual work is conducted in this country by a variety of agencies, including Women's Aid, Refuge and other domestic violence services, the NSPCC, Barnardo's, CAFCASS and so on. One-to-one emotional, and possibly therapeutic, support work with children may be carried out by counsellors, refuge children's workers, children and families services, youth workers, teachers, children's guardians and others. Therapists and counsellors can also be of assistance.

Overall, in direct work to enable children to heal from childhood domestic violence, our informants for this study affirmed that what is needed is to develop models of work informed by strong underlying principles and values in terms of believing in children, of children's empowerment, and of understanding the gender and other dynamics of domestic violence. A basic requirement is, thus, that the practitioner has some experience and training in domestic violence work, makes direct use of relevant toolkits and support materials, and, importantly, is familiar with the power issues, dynamics and impacts of domestic abuse (Hester *et al.* 2007; Mullender *et al.* 2002). Practitioners without an understanding of domestic violence issues may end up confusing and, at worse, re-traumatising the child.

Children may require help to accurately comprehend and make sense of what has occurred, including who is responsible for the violence – and that is not them (Rivett *et al.* 2006). Such realisations will help to prevent distress and negative impacts on self-esteem. However, supporting children through the therapeutic or counselling process may be lengthy and difficult. In therapeutic interventions with children, for example, it may take many months before the child can even start to deal with the issues.

Thus, practitioners need to be prepared and trained. They need to be able to think carefully and sensitively about each child's individual experiences and needs. Creating an emotionally and physically safe environment is essential to facilitate a child's trust and confidence so that they feel able to risk engaging in self-expression and disclosure of painful experiences. This also entails operating within a supportive framework of validation, setting appropriate boundaries and using in-depth emotional work. Practitioners are likely to encounter rage, grief, fear, intense sadness, possible self-destructiveness and other behavioural difficulties in children. The work is hard and it is easy for the worker to be overwhelmed or to get confused as to direction. It is also sometimes the case that the pain and difficulty in dealing with the subject resides with the worker, as opposed to lying with the child. Thus the practitioner needs effective support too.

The basic tenet of any therapeutic or healing process with children is not only the need to start from where the child is, but to ensure that – as children cannot recover from abuse that they continue to experience – they are safe and supported. It is then possible to use a wide variety of methods, including counselling, drawing, art therapy, puppets and possibly group work, as needed. All of this means creating a safe place for the child to be in, where they can begin to explore what has happened to them. It means enabling children to deal with angry and hurt feelings; it means helping them to develop ways to protect themselves and to handle emotional difficulties; and it means standing alongside them as they gradually may be able to become more resilient. Reliable, non-abusive adult allies in this recovery processes are precious and invaluable. Sometimes a parent (often the mother), grandparent or relative can be such an ally, as can a skilled and dedicated practitioner or social worker prepared to put in the time. Quick 'in-and-out' social work interventions are unlikely to be of much help.

Any direct work of this type needs to focus on the actuality of the children's experiences and may include assisting them in dealing with sometimes contradictory feelings of confusion, unhappiness and anger (Hester *et al.* 2007). Children may need to understand that it is acceptable to be angry, but not violent. They may be upset and frightened by their own anger, and both sexes, but boys in particular, may fear that they will become abusive themselves when they grow up (Jaffe *et al.* 1990; Mullender *et al.* 2002). Help with these issues can be crucial in transforming both how children view, and how they feel about, themselves and their future.

Dorota Iwaniec has produced a wide range of literature on emotional abuse of children. She discusses ways to decrease the damage of childhood adversity and general emotional abuse in her useful handbook, *The Emotionally Abused and Neglected Child* (Iwaniec 2006). While Iwaniec considers emotional and adverse experiences in general, rather than childhood experiences of domestic abuse specifically, her discussions are helpful. She emphasises the all-important need to pay attention to the particular vulnerabilities and protective factors pertaining to each emotionally damaged child in order most effectively to enhance resilience (Iwaniec *et al.* 2006). Each child might be different and there is no 'one size fits all' solution.

Iwaniec discusses in detail how the damage done to children can be repaired. The intervention methods she describes include techniques for conducting work with mothers/carers and children together, building secure attachment with non-abusing parents or substitute parents, behavioural work on anger, aggression and conflict resolution, problem sharing and solving with children in practical ways, and the use, where indicated, of cognitive behavioural and motivational interviewing social work approaches. In terms of direct work with children, her comprehensive suggestions also include relaxation and anti-stress training, promoting resilience through assertiveness and social skills training, play therapy, drawing pictures or making masks and discussing them, children's writing of poems, plays or stories and testimonies, and making videos and watching them together (Iwaniec 2006).

She describes a specific technique named the 'jug of loving water' to help children understand their feelings and to find ways forward. In this way of understanding emotional well-being, the metaphorical suggestion is made that everyone is born with such a 'jug' which contains 'loving water'. The jug is then gradually filled more and more with love and warmth and tender feelings from their family and others, as life goes on. It is suggested that children's jugs are depleted by domestic violence. In the therapy, they are enabled to identify this, but also to identify warm feelings and loving experiences. They metaphorically add these experiences of love and tenderness to their 'jug' to enrich it and begin to fill it. As the therapy continues, both recalled memories and new loving events and feelings hopefully begin to fill up the jug again, and the lives of the children are also enriched and enhanced.

Further issues in direct therapeutic and healing work with children

Oaklander (1978) describes a range of methods for working with children which engage their imagination for healing and recovery. She reminds workers and counsellors about the essence of their role in working with children when she states:

> It is up to me to provide the means by which we will open the doors and windows to their inner worlds. I need to provide the means for children to express their inner worlds. I need to provide methods for children to express their feelings, to get what they are keeping guarded inside out into the open, so that together we can deal with this material. In this way a child can make closure, make choices, and lighten the burdens which get heavier and heavier the longer they are carried. (Oaklander 1978, pp.192–3)

Whichever therapeutic models and means are used to facilitate children's recovery, whether psychodynamic, gestalt therapy, cognitive behavioural, humanist, person-centred and Rogerian, or a mix of all these, it nevertheless remains the case that:

> The relationship between the client and worker is the keystone of therapeutic work. The worker offers herself as someone who will think about what the child shows her and try to 'contain' his thoughts, however disturbing and socially unacceptable they may be. (Copley and Forryan 1997, p.17)

The worker's capacity to empathise, think about and respond effectively to what a child expresses, both in and outside the therapeutic space, will be enhanced if she/he has a sound working knowledge, not only of the power dynamics of domestic violence, but also of child development, attachment, defensive coping mechanisms, children's capacity for emotional regulation and the impact of traumatic stress on development. Practitioners now have a wealth of research available to them to enhance knowledge and understanding of the impact of traumatic experiences on all aspects of human development. Space does not allow for a detailed consideration of all available resources. However some referencing may be helpful.

In her studies of childhood trauma Terr (1994) identified a range of psychological defences which children and adults may use to help them cope, including that of dissociation. She found that children who experience what she defines as 'multiple event' trauma (as often occurs in cases of domestic abuse) are most likely to develop dissociation as a coping mechanism and states that: 'abuse and violence at home is the most common setting in which children dissociate' (Terr 1994, p.89). The defensive coping mechanism of dissociation can enable some children to achieve psychologically what cannot be achieved physically, when escape from overwhelmingly frightening and painful experiences is not possible. Achieving 'self-removal' through a form of self-hypnosis can enable the avoidance of abusive experiences and pain, and can reduce, in part or completely, a damaging 'over-dwelling' on what is happening to oneself or in the immediate environment (Terr 1994, p.89). Dissociation can therefore protect the child and facilitate compliance and safety for children in some circumstances where to challenge an abuser would be dangerous and threaten their survival.

The ability to dissociate can be seen to have obvious short-term benefits, but Terr also identifies negative consequences in that:

> A person who uses considerable dissociation does not link up thoughts, behaviours and emotions. Frequently, there is an

alteration in the state of consciousness. Such people may forget or ignore pain. They may forget or ignore parts of their own bodies. They may forget or ignore their own personal history. They may forget or ignore themselves altogether. (Terr 1994, p.69)

Children who need to use dissociation as a way of coping with distress may find that it leads to a wider avoidance of life experiences and also can be triggered by other occurrences and feelings of alarm which remind them of previous experiences. The second author has experience of working directly with children who, for example, have struggled to cope in school when teachers have shown disapproval through shouting, reminding them of their distressing experiences of conflict at home. If children are dissociating in school this will affect their concentration, they may move in and out of awareness and thus have changing levels of ability to retain and recall information. This may result in conflict with educators and/or incorrect evaluations of a child's intellectual capability. Children may fail to achieve their potential if the difficulties they face are not recognised and appropriate support made available to them.

Thus, children's responses may appear deeply confusing to them and to practitioners, unless understood in the context of their intimate experiences and how trauma potentially has an impact on all aspects of development. The need to intervene early is imperative to prevent long-term consequences, bearing in mind that the developmental stage at which an individual is traumatised has a major impact on the degree to which mind and brain are affected. Traumatisation within attachment relationships can have profoundly different impacts on healthy regulation of emotions, self-concept and management of interpersonal relationships than do more 'remote' traumas, for example, disasters and motor vehicle accidents (van der Kolk, MacFarlane and Weisaeth 2007).

Practitioners may find it helpful to refer to texts by van der Kolk *et al.* (2007) and Briere and Scott (2007) for comprehensive information on the subject, including the impact of stress on brain development, and consideration of potential interventions. Additionally, James (1996) has expanded the concept of traumagenic states (emotional conditions arising from traumatic experiences), originally developed by Finkelhor and Browne (1986) in relation to sexual abuse, extending these to nine traumagenic states which may be related more widely to other experiences of trauma and abuse. James describes the dynamics, psychological impacts and behavioural manifestations of these states, which include self-blame, powerlessness, loss and betrayal, and offers guidelines for assessment and intervention (James 1996, p.22).

In a previous text, James (1994) addresses the impact of trauma on attachment relationships, including the development of trauma-bonds. Trauma-bond relationships, possibly with abusive parents or carers, may appear to reflect secure attachments, but actually arise from fear and a child having – for reasons of survival – to seek and maintain proximity to a parent who is dangerous and abusive (James 1994, p.25). Knowledge of trauma-bonds may help to reduce practitioners' confusion about why children may cling to, or request contact with, an abusive parent. This knowledge may – in some circumstances – lead to an increase in effective safeguarding decisions for the protection of children, including more informed questioning relating to parental contact. The impact of domestic and other forms of abuse and neglect on children's development and attachment may lead to affected children being at risk of 'developing disorganised and controlling patterns of attachment' (James 1994, p.198; see also Howe 2005). Understanding this, and the need for support and interventions to enable the development of secure attachments with loving and safe adults who can prioritise their needs, are essential for children's development and for their ability to develop resilience, self-esteem, and the capacity for satisfying relationships with self and others during childhood and later adulthood.

Recognition that 'a whole life can be shaped by an old trauma, remembered or not' (Terr 1994, p.xiii), and that 'every experience a person has in the present is intimately tied to everything that has gone before' (Cattanach 1994, p.57), makes it compelling for a child's behaviour to be considered in the context of her or his previous, as well as current, circumstances, and therefore for the worker to have a detailed understanding of the child's history. In addition to drawing on the records of professional agencies, children's (safe) carers – usually mothers – may be willing to provide information about significant events and changes in a child's life – both positive and negative – from pre- and post-birth to the present time. The second author has previously undertaken such work with mothers using pictorial images (for example road maps) and timelines for this purpose. Such techniques, and associated discussion about a family's history, not only provide opportunities to deepen the worker's understanding and capacity to relate to a child's experiences, they may also facilitate a parent's deeper understanding of their child's development and an ability to make sense of their emotional and behavioural responses and needs.

Although this work may be painful for (non-abusing) parents, it can also result, if carried out in a supportive manner, in feelings of empowerment as a result of the parent knowing that they are making an important and creative contribution to a successful outcome of therapy and to their child's recovery. This can lead parents to greater awareness and acceptance of the need for therapeutic work, which is vital if they are to feel confident and able to give their child clear permission to talk about anything they may wish to with the worker. If such permission is withheld, children who have previously been expected to keep the domestic abuse a secret may feel they have to continue to do so, and this is likely to be counterproductive to their recovery.

There should also be an assessment to consider the capacity of the parent to support their child through the therapeutic process and to cope with the inevitable changes and challenges this will present, as the child begins working through painful feelings and experiences, with additional support identified for the parent where needed. In some situations, it may be possible to identify other sources of support, in addition to the parent, that may be available to the child during the therapeutic process (for example, support from another family member, teacher or social worker, related beneficial activities, and so on).

Children may have ideas about what ought to happen and the assistance they need, and may choose to communicate the worries or feelings with which they would like help. Where this is the case, the worker is obligated to try to address them, rather than pursuing a different agenda. However, due to the impact of their experiences, children may also experience post-traumatic stress disorder, as discussed in previous chapters, and struggle to comprehend or to articulate their concerns. With or without these difficulties, children should know that they have choices and will not be forced to talk about anything that they do not wish to. Children should also be helped to understand what the boundaries are in relation to the privacy of their therapeutic sessions, including who will be given information about the content and what will happen if any disclosures or safeguarding concerns arise. These matters can all be made part of the agreement between the worker, child and parent/carer at the beginning of the direct work, and reviewed at regular intervals to address any changes that may be necessary. Child-centred agreements and review processes which value and encourage the expression of children's wishes and feelings, and – what is important – actively address them, can provide a powerful and positive contradiction to earlier negative experiences of the power and control dynamics of domestic abuse.

Workbooks and further activities

Various texts exist, such as those discussed in this chapter, which may enhance practitioner knowledge, skills, confidence and sensitivity in their approaches to supporting children affected by domestic abuse. Some specifically focused practical resources also now exist geared to children's exposure to domestic abuse. These resources attempt to enable mothers, children and professionals to work constructively together to assist children and young people on a path to recovery. A pioneering example has been provided by Cathy Humphreys, Ravi Thiara, Agnes Skamballis and Audrey Mullender, who have developed a short series of picture and written workbooks (the *Talking to my Mum* materials and guides) about how to enable care-givers/mothers and children to talk together about domestic violence. There are separate books for children and young people. The workbooks present activities, exercises, cartoons and games that may be helpful to practitioners and parents/carers, as well as to children and young people themselves (Humphreys *et al.* 2006).

All of these materials were developed with the direct participation of mothers and children who had experienced domestic abuse, and were part of an action project that involved working with both the mothers and the children to enable them to better understand themselves and their emotions, their interactions and the impact of the domestic abuse on each other. (To use such resources, child participants need to be at a receptive stage of understanding and personal development, and some young people may have moved to a maturity level where workbooks of this type are unnecessary or could appear patronising. Thus, careful and age-appropriate use is to be recommended, as for all helping techniques and interventions.)

Other resources exist on the internet and in self-help books and recovery guides. It is not possible to investigate all of the available therapeutic tools and resources in detail in this short account. Whatever the methods, however, there is a need to be led by the child and young person, to listen and affirm, to go at their speed and to be sure that at all times they feel safe and secure. It is all too easy, as noted throughout, to impose such work and solutions on children who have possibly already been made compliant by their abuse experiences, so that they lose control of the process in a way which can be unhelpful and, at worst, re-victimising (see also Hester *et al.* 2007).

Group work

Since the early 1990s, group work sessions with groups of young people who have experienced domestic violence have been used. These programmes of group work have developed to a considerable extent in Canada and the United States (see Hague *et al.* 2001). They developed somewhat later in the UK where they are usually run by refuge organisations and domestic violence services, or by children's charities such as Barnardo's or the NSPCC. Sometimes individual work with children can lead on to group sessions if this seems appropriate, or both can occur together.

Group work manuals and programmes of how to conduct such work on domestic violence issues exist, especially in North America, and can be bought in to assist and advise new programmes. One of the most respected is the Ontario model, offering groups for children aged 4 to 16 years, which has been replicated in some places in the UK. These groups deal with naming and understanding the abuse and children's feelings about it, coping constructively with anger and aggression, keeping safe, accessing social support, helping each other, understanding oneself and family relationships, understanding men's violence to women, and looking at who is responsible for individual behaviour (Hague *et al.* 2001; Wilson *et al.* 1986). Some Canadian programmes are run with substantial input and control by groups of young people themselves in schools and youth groups.

It has been suggested that such groups work best where the child's experiences of abuse have been mild to moderate (Jaffe *et al.* 1990). In severe cases, one-to-one work is necessitated. Sometimes children can also find attending specialist groups stigmatising and prefer that the issues addressed be less clearly about domestic abuse, possibly cover some wider matters, and are not identifiable by the group's name or in any publicity. Where these sensitive issues can be addressed, children attending such groups often think they are a good idea and can be enthusiastic about them (Hague *et al.* 2001; Mullender *et al.* 2002). They can talk, share and learn from each other, and often enjoy moments of group hilarity.

In fact, in a children's group in a refuge facilitated by the main author, hilarity of this type resulted in people having to fall over and roll on the floor, but serious issues were also broached and examined together (in a slightly chaotic way). The group concluded with the following insights:

> We cope in all sorts of different ways. But lots of children are good at it… They don't necessarily get upset and in a state about it. They

can do fine with it. Some do get upset and they need support and caring because it is such a big thing. It is definitely really a big thing for children… Grown-ups don't realise sometimes because they are always going on about their stuff and they forget that the children might be hurt too…

They also contributed insightful stories and explained how the support of other children can be of key importance in building a new life. Peer support and helping each other were the things they believed in more than anything else.

In more detail: how do the groups work?

Prerequisites for attending a group programme are usually that the child is living in a safe environment and no longer with the perpetrator of the domestic violence. All groups do an assessment of children referred to assess whether the experience will be suitable. Both the child and the mother must then give consent, and the child must be happy to attend and not feel coerced. There needs to be a dedicated attempt to minimise any possible stigmatisation for the child or young person as a result of attending, as noted above. A safe and supportive venue needs to be available, possibly away from the child's usual environs and not publicly known in their social friendship or school circles.

Even so, some children may be too embarrassed to attend such groups and may be fearful of their friends finding out, or just somehow 'knowing'. Sensitivity is essential in dealing with these issues of confidentiality, embarrassment and the important understanding that groups are only suitable for some children and, even then, perhaps not consistently so. It is clearly not appropriate to make children talk about domestic violence if they do not want to do so in groups, just as in individual work.

Mothers also might need support to feel confident that the fact that their child is participating in group work (or, indeed, individual work) is going to be helpful and is not personally threatening or incriminating. Both mothers and children might fear that the groups will lead to them being adversely judged by each other, and by other children or adults in the group, and that embarrassing or previously confidential and deeply personal issues might be shared which reflect badly on them. This is clearly an issue for mothers, but can be for participating children or their siblings too.

Thus, privacy and confidentiality are essential for all children's groups. The expectation is always that they are facilitated by trained adults, and are conducted in a way which is culturally aware in terms of diversity and equality. Sessions might use supportive materials, play activities and physical or creative means of expression, as well as verbal communication, and be able to be used by disabled or Deaf children if needed. Likely issues to be addressed for participants include talking about what domestic abuse is in a sensitive way, expressing and understanding their feelings, dealing with anger and distress, exploring safety and ways of protecting themselves and that they are not to blame, and building healthy relationships. The content may be developed and agreed by, and with, the young people themselves, as well as the ground rules.

An evaluation of early groups in the USA found that children thought that they had been broadly helpful in bringing their experiences out into the open and beginning to address them, although all children responded differently (Peled and Edleson 1992). A very shy or sensitive child might feel threatened and overwhelmed, for example. Some children in this evaluation had refused to speak with their mothers about the group, preferring to keep the experience private. While this outcome may be important for an individual child, however, interactions with mothers can be constructive to help with addressing the issues raised. In many groups, children are encouraged to talk about the group with their mothers, whose role can be crucial in supporting them through the experience (see also Hester *et al.* 2007).

UK groups

As a result of these types of issues, there have been some successful groups set up in the UK where the mothers and children meet in their own separate groups at the same time and then everyone joins together afterwards, perhaps for lunch or snacks. The planned group sessions may have been tied in together so that mothers and children can share their feelings and insights afterwards if they choose to. Critically, the mothers' sessions may include assistance and support in how to handle issues that may have come up for their children and how to support them adequately in dealing with the group experiences. This can include supporting the children and young people with precipitated memories of abuse, new insights gained, or feelings about perpetrators. The latter may include anger and hurt, but also perhaps loving and missing them, particularly where the abuser is also their father.

In one UK group programme with which the authors interacted, there is an initial assessment, and then children attend up to 12 sessions which include review meetings. The sessions are structured and run in partnership (but confidentially) with relevant schools. Most programmes of this type are friendly and flexible and may be led by 'explorers'. Some cover a laid-down structured programme. Barnardo's, for example, run a particularly wide range of groups around the country for children experiencing domestic violence, including for very young children, with carefully worked out programmes and sensitive facilitation.

In another group investigated by the authors and run by a different organisation, up to eight children aged seven to eleven who have been affected by domestic abuse attend for ten weeks, and may have an attached confidential mentor at school. The group provides a safe and welcoming environment in which children feel safe enough to explore and share some of their experiences of domestic abuse. Methods include games, stories, films, puppets, painting and drawing. Programmes of this type address low confidence levels and self-esteem, poor sleep/eating patterns, self-blame, limited networks of friends, aggressive or disruptive behaviour and emotions of sadness, anger and loneliness. Most groups start with an initial orientation. Some UK group are ostensibly about other issues to avoid young people having to see themselves as domestic violence victims, and may cover healthy relationships and relationship issues more broadly, as discussed for groups more generally above. A few groups for children exposed to domestic abuse also now exist specifically for children and young people with challenging behaviour and other difficulties. Thus, a great deal of expertise now exists across the UK about children's group work in cases of domestic violence, and advice and resources are available to assist those starting new groups.

In this chapter, we have discussed a variety of methods with which practitioners and agencies can engage in direct work with children to enable positive adult outcomes. There are many ways to work with children from domestically violent households to enable them to deal with their experiences in appropriate ways and to recover as adults. The various initiatives and ways of working that we have discussed may be of help to practitioners, social workers, child psychologists, refuge children's workers and policy-makers, but also may assist domestic abuse survivors directly in moving forward to a future where both children and adults are less damaged by abusive childhood experiences of domestic violence than at present. Ways of working with adults who have witnessed domestic abuse as children, the main focus of this book, are discussed at some length in Chapter 8.

In the next chapter, 'Anna', a pseudonym, describes graphically her childhood experiences of domestic violence, the long-term impacts of these experiences, and how she struggled towards ultimate recovery. She then goes on to present helpful ideas to assist others to also move forward.

Chapter 7

Still Hurting

Testimony by 'Anna'

How to explain to others why I am often not comfortable in my skin and why do I apologise for mostly everything I do? When will I have confidence in the real 'me'? Coming from an unconventional educational background, I recently completed my degree as a mature student at a top university, but feel disappointed with myself for getting a good Upper Second, rather than a First. Perhaps, I still try to overcompensate or even worse withdraw, go inwards. Still, I am getting stronger.

I guess I need to go back, back to a world of unpredictability. A world where the skills that make me seem sometimes strange today may very well have saved my life. By this, I mean hyper-vigilance. As a child I *had* to read the signs, the sounds, smells, tone and body language. The smell of cider on his breath – even today that smell pulls me back. 'Domestic violence': thanks to the work of many, it has now become less of a taboo subject. Some of this has occurred, due to the work of the activists of the 1970s, a movement that began before I was born, but things have moved on greatly since then.

When I was a child in the early 1980s, many of the neighbours were kind to me. I remember meeting 'kind' adults, and sometimes I would wish they would take me home. I remember going to other children's houses (friends from school) and wanting to stay there and to never leave – I remember that feeling of safety, of being able to be a child, of just being myself. I know that everyone grows up thinking that other families were somehow better than theirs, or 'normal' – but that feeling of being in safe places almost made it worse when I had to return. I remember times when things were really good when I was a child, but, if I am honest, there are really only two proper memories of happy times from when we lived with him – the 'master', my dad. This is not just over-statement. At one point, he actually called himself 'the master' and sat in a tatty antique chair he called 'the throne'. We, also, were expected to call him 'the master'. It sounds almost silly writing this now at the age of 31, but back then he really was our master.

I tried so hard to get things right as a child. I so desperately wanted to do what I felt he wanted. I did this at all times, because, at any moment, he could change. There were some signs that made it clear that there would be trouble, such as losing a horse racing bet or coming home drunk or on drugs. At these times at least, we knew what was coming; still, at other times we had no idea. I remember a clear example of when I tried really hard to do something to please my father. I think I was around ten years old. My dad had been badly beaten, and his face was swollen, cut and bruised. He had gone out the day before and got drunk; this was our fault, which I will explain later. Anyway, we were sat outside in the garden, and my dad was drinking cans of larger, something strong like Special Brew or Tenants Super. He had finished his can over ten minutes before and was obviously in pain from the beating he had received, so I went to the fridge and got him another can. I was sure this would please him. But when I went to give it to him, I saw his face change, it became red and his top lip began to tighten. I knew then that he was angry and I had no idea why.

'Are you trying to make me look like a fucking alcoholic, playing mind games? I know what you are trying to do', my dad hissed at me.

As a small child, these times were the worst; I would cry and run away. Later, I can remember times in school when I got into trouble as a teenager. It was always the same kind of thing, for example if a teacher shouted really loudly at me out of the blue or suddenly. It brought back memories to me in a panic. I was bullied at school, during and after we left my dad's house. I was nervous and had no self-esteem – we had no money to buy new clothes at the time, and my dad had taken our belongings and had then had a mysterious fire in which they were all burnt. Still, in the grand scheme of things I did not care.

Going back to when I was younger, we should not have even been at that house. We had escaped to a women's refuge the night before, but my mum had taken us back. I am not angry at my mum for returning, she was brave to take us there in the first place. Unless you've lived in a house like ours, you cannot imagine the mind games our father played. That time when we did go to the refuge for one night, it was amazing. I do not remember it being particularly new or clean looking, but it was safe and that was the most important thing. There was even a children's playroom and in it were toys, books and a bouncy castle. Once again, for that day, we played and were children. I bounced all day on the bouncy castle. Sadly, though, it was only for one day and night. Somehow, my auntie (my dad's sister) spoke with my mum and told her about how her brother (my dad) had been terribly beaten up. Never mind how many times we had been beaten by him. Of course, it was due to the stress of us leaving; she said that he had got blind drunk, taken off his clothes and flashed on top of a bridge, until he eventually got beaten up by a group of men. The story did the trick for my mum, and we were back there.

I know my dad blamed me for us all going to the refuge. He had been warning me about talking to my social worker, and he had never been able to trust me after I had phoned the police at the age of eight or nine. I remember that day so clearly – perhaps these are the reasons I still find it hard to trust anyone. I heard banging, shouting and my mum crying. I ran downstairs to see my dad down on the floor on his knees with his face close to my mum's. My mum was crying and her face looked red and puffy. My dad had photos of her parents (who were both dead) and was threatening to tear them up and shouting. Mum tried to get the photos from my dad, and he threw her down on the floor. I ran towards him, but it was futile, he pushed me across the room so easily. Something snapped that day, and I ran out of the house and down the hill until I reached the main road. Once I had crossed over via the green man, I went into the phone box and dialled 999 without hesitating. When the operator answered, I explained that my dad was hurting me and my mum and we needed help. I told them the address and she said I should wait outside my house. I remember I said I was too scared to go back and that he would hurt me when he found out I had called the police. The woman was kind and we arranged for me to meet the police in a car park near the house.

When they arrived in their police car – two tall, strong policemen wearing official uniforms – I felt relief. We were going to be safe now. I told the police about the incident that had happened that day and about many more. They asked me to come into the house with them, but I said there was no way, that I was too scared. So they went to the house, while I hid in the back of the police car. My heart was pounding as I lay flat on the back seat of the car. What if he came running out to find me? I couldn't even get out of the car now, and he could smash the window. After what seemed like a very long time, the two officers came back to the car. One of them opened the car door and held out his hand to gesture for me to come out. He said 'Come on, let's get you inside' (or something like that). I asked where my dad was, the policeman explained that he was inside waiting to talk to me. I pleaded with them not to take me back inside, but one of them said 'Sorry love, this is a domestic matter, something to be sorted out between you and your dad; no one is angry with you'. At this point everything changed for me; I lost a lot of hope that day. The 'big strong policemen' whom I was brave enough to call did not protect me. What was worse was that my dad knew that he had more control than ever. We were alone in that house, and my dad, who was often in a drug- and alcohol-induced psychosis, could do whatever he wanted with us. When I got older I disliked the police for a long time – it took me a while to connect my experience of them at eight and the feeling of being terribly let down.

When I got slightly older, I began to spend as much time as possible outside of the house. So, at the age of nine, when my dad threw my mum out of the house – another example of his control that was a frequent occurrence – I decided to go with her. I quickly put my roller skates on and skated after my mum down a rather steep hill. It was not until I reached the bottom of the hill that I started to catch up with her. Unfortunately, this was also the point where my dad caught up with me.

He grabbed me by my pony tail and dragged me back up the steep hill by my hair. When we reached the top of the hill and got back inside the house, he grabbed a rolling pin and hit me as hard as he could across my bottom. To this day, that was the most intense pain I have experienced, it slammed against bone. The bruise lasted for weeks, and, as I had been going outside of the house more, it came to someone's attention. An older boy, or young man, called Pete, used to work on cars outside of the front of where we lived. Once he told me to check for something under the bonnet of his car and beeped the horn really loud. I think he saw how scared I was and how unsure as to whether it had been a joke or he was going to hurt me. So, when he saw me go to sit down and then jump back up, he must have noticed I was in pain. He asked me to show him what was hurting and for some reason I did. Nothing happened really at the time, but later that night I heard a terrible noise and my mum screaming and crying 'leave him alone', 'at least fight him one at a time'. She sounded so desperate. Then I heard Pete's voice, 'I know what he has been doing to Anna, she's a little kid, let him pick on someone his own size'. That night they beat him up, some of them had baseball bats. I was not satisfied, I was scared, because I knew one of us, or all of us, would pay for me speaking out again.

Other times, the abuse would be more psychological. I think we were all so scared and withdrawn by a certain point that the threat of violence was enough to control us. One time, my dad came home late at night in a strange mood; he may have taken drugs, who knows. He said we were all going have a spiritual experience and all learn how to be closer to God. He was near to another mental breakdown at this point. First, he said we had to sit and meditate. We knew the lotus position and we all sat down as instructed, while Dad led a chant. If my father wanted to have a spiritual experience, then we were not going to go to bed until he had one. After meditating for a while, he asked me to look into his eyes, to really look deep into his eyes and tell him what I saw. What was I supposed to tell him? He was so unpredictable, and when I looked in his eyes all I felt was fear, all I saw was the man who tortured me and the people I loved. Still, I could not say that, so I lied, I told him what I thought he wanted to hear. I was afraid, afraid that he could see deep into my own eyes and that he would know all I saw was blackness. I kept looking deep into his eyes composing myself, thinking so carefully of what the right thing to say might be and then I told him: 'I see the ocean and it is vast and endless and I feel peace like being by the sea'.

This worked, he seemed pleased with my lie, but I hated myself. Why could I not say the truth, tell him what I really thought? Of course, I knew he would hurt us if I did. Next, he wanted us to see him do a headstand, and he actually seemed in a better mood. He kept trying to do it and then would fall over and laugh; we were laughing too. Then he got angry and said it was serious and that no one would go to bed until he had done his headstand. It sounds almost ridiculous now, writing about it, that he had so much control over all of us. We were like playthings, and after the pub that night he wanted to play with us all night long. We were awake for hours past our bedtime; each time he fell I became more scared, and he became more frustrated. For me, the unpredictability of his behaviour affected me the most. This is what I have found hardest in my life as an adult. I have to keep telling myself I am safe now: I do not need to be on the lookout for danger, I can trust people.

For me, the trouble started in my own behaviour only once we were safe. I was so used to walking on eggshells and trying to be perfect that, when I no longer had to because of my dad, I rebelled at the age of 13 to 14. When we first left my dad's control, school bullies took his place. We were vulnerable. There was never any support to help us come to terms with the trauma. Knowing what I do now about the effects of abuse, I feel our whole family were suffering from post-traumatic stress disorder (PTSD). I cannot complain about the refuge we later went to because, without it, we would never have escaped. It is true, though, that there were issues with violence within the refuge. For example, on the first day of our second stay at the refuge (which was nine months altogether), a woman came running into our bedroom and attacked my mother over the bed on which I was sitting. As it happens, they later managed to become good friends.

However, issues with violence are not surprising considering the normalisation of abuse to which these families had been subject. Nevertheless, I do not remember any other violence between the adults in the refuge, and there were true friendships made in that place that we came to call home. When we were in the refuge, we were all just so happy to be safe. One thing I remember clearly is all the lovely food we had to eat. Now the money was in my mum's name, she would spend most of it on food shopping. It sounds silly but having yoghurts, biscuits, squash, breakfast, lunch and dinner every day were luxuries. When we lived with my dad, he had control of the money and he had issues with most addictions; his favourites were alcohol, drugs and gambling. I remember giro day. My dad was always so happy on that fortnightly occasion.

Sometimes my dad let us go with him to cash the giro and he would then buy us a treat. I was too young to understand some of the games, and it was not until I grew up that I did. Once, he cashed the giro and gave me £1. I thought it was a lot so I must have been young. He gave it to me and said 'Tell your mum to make it last'. So, off I ran to give it to my mum not knowing the full implications – he had taken the rest of the money meant for two weeks and left my mum with nothing. My dad kept financial control over my mum because all the benefits were in his name. I remember being hungry so much; sometimes I could not sleep due to an empty stomach.

My mum was a brave and loving woman. Throughout everything she loved us. My dad tried to make us turn against her, to make us say terrible things, but he could never do it. He always blamed her for what he did, how he acted – he brought up her worst mistakes all the time. I know that my dad was a sick and controlling man, and I had a social worker for most of the time I lived with him – but I guess things were different back then. It is when I remember back to those days that I am in awe of the amazing work that has been done in the field of domestic abuse.

Sometimes, though, it is the after-effects which cut the deepest, when the numbness subsides and it is safe enough to feel – then the real fight begins. When this happened for me, we were alone as a family and had left my dad. My mum was a single parent dealing with four children, all with their own separate problems, stemming from the mental and physical torture and violence we had endured at his hands. When we arrived in our flat in a new town after the refuge, and where we knew nobody, it was very scary. He came to our new safe house and there was no one for me to tell. The one good thing about where we had moved was that my uncle and auntie did not live far away. They were safe, I knew. They had encouraged Mum to leave my dad and helped her get a few items from the old house before he burnt it.

After a few weeks of him being back, he was hurting Mum again and spitting in her face. I remember I stood up to him – sort of. I ran upstairs and Mum came up asked me what was wrong. I said, 'I don't want him here'. I did not feel safe. Then, he came to me and confronted me. I told him how I felt, and he said that it was my fault and that I was destroying the family, that I would deny my brother a father if I made him leave. This was such a heavy burden that I still feel today. I ran all the way to my uncle's house and they protected me. Luckily, when I returned the next day, Dad was gone and he never came back.

The after-effects

When my dad left, my mum already had four children, I was the only girl and having three brothers was sometimes difficult. During the years we had lived with my dad, we children had all been close, particularly me and my slightly older brother. On Sundays, we had gone to church together, just me and my big brother. He would hold my hand and look after me. It makes me sad to think that our relationship turned so bad, once we were both teenagers, though our relationship is great again now. As an adult, I can see why we then psychologically and even sometimes physically attacked each other so violently: we were following a pattern. In fact, violence and shouting carried on at my mum's house for a while after we left, as the legacy of my dad lived on in a way that has been so difficult to break. Instead of talking things through, issues seem to build up and spill out, in the extreme through violent acts of slamming doors, and punching holes in doors. Sometimes, I think that my youngest brothers don't know why they are so very angry. It is as if, once we finally left my dad, everybody stopped talking about what had happened. But, for the youngest two brothers, I wonder whether they understand exactly where their frustration stems from.

Now that I am older, I question the support available for my family when we 'got away' from my dad and the domestic abuse. We were re-housed, which is not a small thing, and I am still so grateful that we could physically escape from my dad, thanks to the refuge. However, there was just no support for us as children. We were, I think, on the child protection register for a time. I do remember having to be weighed and have meetings with the school nurse about my feelings and situation. Still, it seemed like my mum somehow had to find the strength to suddenly have all the skills necessary to be a good single mum of four children, in a strange place, when she and all four of us had experienced such terrible physical and psychological abuse. If I could go back to that time, I would want my mum to go on the current *Freedom Programme* which is an empowering programme for survivors of domestic abuse – where she could build confidence and understand what had happened to her. Because she felt a great deal of shame and guilt, she tried so hard to make it up to us in the best way she knew, but she really did not know what to do. I am sure, if my mum could go back, she would do things very differently, too.

We now have a strong family unit. Things are not perfect – but my mum has spent her time, from when we left my dad until this very day, making our lives better. She has built a safe home, where there is always love, food, warmth, and many more of the things we had lacked in the past. Perhaps my mum going back to university was one of the factors that inspired me to do the same. Though there are issues in our family, we can now talk about the effects of 'back then' and we love and support each other.

Some ways that childhood domestic abuse affects adults

This short account cannot do justice to the multiple forms of abuse I experienced on an ongoing basis as a child from my father. As an adult it took me a long time to even recognise the effects of the abuse. Trust is perhaps my biggest issue, and a sense of feeling that I am on the outside. Many other survivors have also talked with me about feeling marginalised, an outsider, not trusting anyone, having no self-confidence and feeling a constant failure. The impacts don't go away easily.

Leading from this is the desire to always please people, to always try and do things 'right', but it still feel as though you never do get it right. Then, as an adult, there is the challenge of trying to build your own healthy and positive relationships with a lack of these examples in your own experience. That is not to say that all people who experience domestic abuse will then become abusive, or not be able to have healthy relationships, but to recognise that in a closed unit such as the family, abuse can sometimes become normalised and that it can take some work to undo this. That is why programmes such as the *Freedom Programme* (www.freedomprogramme.co.uk/) are so useful. They help survivors to understand what a healthy loving relationship looks like, and also to make sense of their past experience. The website offers online resources, meaning that anyone with safe access to the internet can use them, and also has details of programmes people can attend across the country.

Though there are times that I lack confidence in myself, it is important for me to realise how far I have come. I am lucky that I have had so many amazing people in my life who have made a difference to my journey. I am also honoured that with their love and support and my own strength, I have managed to survive, physical, emotional and sexual abuse. Of course there are days when I feel low, but most of us have those days. It is about having the support and resources to get through those days. People can heal, and even grow. I know that I have.

How do we heal from the effects of domestic violence as adults?

There is much more support out there now for people who have experienced domestic violence than when I was young. Depending on where you are in the country, there is access to many different types of services. Much of the support available relates directly to helping people to escape from current domestic abuse situations, which of course is vital. However, from my own later work experience in supporting people who have experienced domestic abuse, regardless of ethnicity, whether they be male, female, heterosexual, LBGT (lesbian, gay, bi-sexual and trans gendered), impaired or able bodied; there seem to be fewer services available once you have left an abusive situation, particularly as time goes on. When you consider the effects on children who experience domestic violence, these effects are likely also to be carried on into adulthood.

Today, there is more support out there for children who witness and/ or experience domestic violence than in the past, but still not enough. The Women's Aid's website for children affected by domestic abuse is one example of the positive steps forward that have taken place since I was in a refuge, first in 1989 and then in 1991. The website known as The Hideout (www.thehideout.org.uk, see Hideout 2011) provides a safe space for children and young people to attempt to understand and even to come to terms with what has happened to them and their families. There are two formats that the website comes in, depending on the age of the person viewing it: webpages for a) children and b) young people. The language is therefore accessible. There are clear definitions of what abuse is, and there are real stories that come in the form of videos. This is great as it allows children and young people to be able to feel less isolated and/or alone.

For help with domestic violence, people can now contact the Freephone 24-hour National Domestic Violence Helpline on 0808 2000 247. This 24-hour helpline not only gives information on refuge availability, but also has lists of all services relating to domestic violence across the country, and is an invaluable resource of support and advice. Victim Support is a national charity which helps those who have experienced any crime (see www.victimsupport.com/Contact-us). They have specialists in the area of domestic violence, and can help men and women with the effects of domestic abuse. The funding of specialist Independent Domestic Violence Advisers (IDVAs) illustrates the government's commitment to support men, women and children who have experienced domestic abuse.

Other very helpful resources provided by Women's Aid are the *Survivor's Forum* and *Survivor's Handbook* – online resources offering advice on many aspects of domestic abuse and its impact. There is an excellent section for parents in the *Survivor's Handbook* on how to support their children after leaving a domestic abuse partnership, and sections for anyone who has experienced domestic violence. Some of the web resources are interactive and are available now, through social networking sites, as well as refuge, support, outreach and advocacy domestic violence services. I strongly advocate that anyone experiencing abuse, but especially children and young people, makes use of these services. There are resources out there that can help you. Further information on ways to recover from experiences of domestic abuse as children and how professionals can help are available in other chapters of this book.

Chapter 8

How to Move Forward

*Recovery, Assistance and Support
for Adults with Childhood
Experiences of Domestic Abuse*

> Well, it has dominated my life. I feel that my childhood was destroyed.
> I can remember feeling happy and confident before I found out about
> it. Then there was the hiding, pretending it didn't happen. Never letting
> anyone know. Feeling so mortified… I never knew it happened to
> anyone else. It's made me manipulative, secretive, lacking in self-respect,
> unable to complete my own healthy development, emotionally scarred,
> and guilty all the time – unable to face the world squarely and say I
> have a place in it. (Adult daughter, interviewed in Hague and Wilson
> 1996, p.37)

Following on from the moving testimony in the previous chapter and in
the quote above, this chapter builds on the discussions in Chapter 6, which
considered direct work which may assist children to heal from experiences
of domestic violence. We concentrate in this chapter specifically on
recovery work with adults, both women and men, and address ways in
which those struggling with such childhood experiences may be able
to get help and move forward. The chapter adopts a similar structure to
Chapter 6, moving through discussions of general issues, resilience, the
insights of our informants and their advice to others, practice issues to
assist recovery, and specific healing or counselling techniques that agencies
and survivors themselves can use.

As the testimonies from 'Rose Wood' in Chapter 5 and 'Anna' in
Chapter 7 make clear, the journey to recovery for adults who experienced
domestic abuse as children is long, convoluted and difficult. Quite often,
it is replete with unhappiness, setbacks and emotional relapses. Adult
survivors talk about ongoing pain and often self-recrimination, as though
what had happened was their personal fault, even though they may know
rationally that it was not. 'Anna' in her testimony describes constantly

feeling to blame, and how easy it is, even in adulthood, for circumstances suddenly to knock her back to self-contempt and her abusive past. She can never achieve enough to satisfy herself. Another older survivor spoke of everything that she had not yet achieved seeming wonderful, superior and important. At the same time, everything she had already achieved felt like unimportant nonsense. This was the case for the same achievement. It would morph from wonderful and enviable when others had achieved it, to nothing – as soon as she herself had achieved it.

Many survivors of domestic abuse in childhood also talk of feeling more or less fine for a while, maybe years, and thinking that maybe they have successfully left it all behind. Then suddenly something happens that sends them skidding down a spiral back to emotional self-destructiveness, confusion, pain and anguish. For some, these periodic spirals continue throughout life.

Setbacks, personal pain and sadness pervade this life territory. It can be helpful for those in the situation attempting to make changes to recognise that such setbacks are very likely to be part of the process, and not a cause for 'beating yourself up'. Nevertheless, this is often what happens. Survivors of abuse of this type are often particularly good at putting themselves down, deriding themselves and dwelling on their failures. While this is true of most survivors of abuse of all types, it can be exacerbated for those with childhood domestic violence experiences as they may feel that they do not have a real 'reason' to be affected, unlike, say, those who experienced severe childhood sexual abuse. After all, they were (in many cases) not directly abused themselves, so what are they making so much fuss about it? Since others seem to get by without ill effects, why can't they? What is wrong with them? This short poem was written for the main author by a 33-year-old woman with domestic violence experiences as a child, named 'Shaila' (pseudonym):

WHAT IS WRONG WITH ME?
What is wrong with me?
How can I be so pathetic?
I've got nothing to complain about.
My childhood is long gone.
So what am I going on about?
How weak and tragic am I.
I just can't get over it.
It keeps coming back.
How stupid is that?

Unnecessary.
Pathetic.
Get over it, girl.
But I can't.
Tragic.

'Shaila' kept finding that life was getting better, only to fall into depression or to sabotage her own happiness, and then to feel self-loathing as a result. Like the experiences of adults in the focus group discussed in Chapter 4 and in the testimonies, the memories for 'Shaila' kept coming back, and she felt that she was unable to become a proper mature, balanced person, which made her feel even worse about herself.

This book is about reassuring those in this situation that experiencing domestic abuse as a child is indeed a trauma and that it is a reasonable human reaction to be distressed in adulthood. It is not a lesser form of adverse experience that, as 'Shaila' says, you should be able to 'get over', but cannot. The book aims to assist survivors to 'own' the validity, depth and distress of their experiences and emotional reactions, and to avoid minimising them – or feeling a failure for even having them. As our informant, 'Rose Wood', points out, a childhood scarred by domestic abuse often means that children have grown up in a situation where they are not being protected by either parent (for example, if their mother is dis-enabled by the violence, and the father is perhaps sequentially absent or abusive). Thus, they may be left in a terrifying and emotionally catastrophic situation, which, further, they may well be forbidden from talking about, so that it becomes an onerous secret and burden.

Such a childhood is likely to result in the adult experiencing a heavy and sometimes treacherous impact, with long-term effects. Adult survivors being able to recognise this, and coming to understand that their experiences of childhood domestic violence can be as traumatic, important and deserving of attention as are those of other abuse survivors, can be a giant step in recovering. The sense of relief on reaching these realisations can, according to our respondents, be huge. It can even be transforming for some, leading to feeling personally worthwhile and at some sort of peace.

Thus a major aim of this chapter is to assist people in the situation to recognise, validate and stop feeling guilty about their own experiences – rather than often deriding them. It also aims to point the way forward in how to recover, understand – forgive perhaps – and come to a point of personal resolution. Further, it aims to offer recommendations, guidance and suggestions for working on this issue for professionals and agencies. In this, it starts to fill a gap or, at least, makes a contribution to recognising that such a gap exists. Help for adults who have experienced domestic violence as children, both men and women, has tended to be sidelined within abuse services up to now, in comparison with work on other forms of childhood abuse and maltreatment. The issues involved have largely escaped both professional attention in general, and (in terms of therapy) the counselling, or psychotherapeutic, gaze for too long.

A glimpse into the past

In the past in the UK, the issues around the effects of domestic violence on children were not addressed at all. The main author interviewed, in 1996, women who had experienced domestic violence between 1945 and 1970 (Hague and Wilson 1996; Hague 2000). In a study called *The Silenced Pain*, these older women, approaching the end of their lives, spoke movingly of the domestic abuse that they had experienced as adults – but also, what is important, as children. For many of them, their interviews were the first time that they had ever spoken of their experiences. In a short book based on the study, Hague and Wilson described the strong and humbling impacts these disclosures had on them as interviewers. Speaking of their interviewees, they wrote:

> Though their lives were drawing to an end, their accounts and their visible distress and hurt attest to the long-lasting and profound effects of domestic violence... We became more and more deeply and painfully aware of the great tragedy that had imbued (their) lives and which, even now, refused to go away. We felt both humbled and privileged to have been given a glimpse into their lives in the distant past... to acknowledge the wide extents and the depth of the hidden and silenced pain. (Hague and Wilson 1996, p.40)

Since then, most of the interviewees have died. The hurt and damage accompanied them to their deaths, such is the power and pain of domestic violence. A few of their children, then in their 40s or 50s, were also interviewed for the study, and spoke of the enduring pain from their own childhoods, as in the following quote, and also in the one which starts this chapter.

> Although I am middle-aged now, I've never forgotten it. It made it more difficult to 'grow up', to separate from them like you should do. Because there was never any space for me to do that, everything was them and the rows and violence. Probably not two days go by when I don't think about it. (Adult daughter, interviewed in Hague and Wilson 1996, p.38)

Now in the 2010s, they too have continued to carry their pain (when contacted for this book) as they approach old age themselves. This book hopes to be part of breaking that process of ongoing pain and ensuring that such life-long tragedy, from childhood on, becomes a thing of the past.

Resilience again

How, then, can depressed, sad or traumatised adults with domestic abuse histories as children address their experiences and begin to recover? Theories of resilience, as discussed in the previous chapter on direct work with children, may be of help. To reiterate, resilience is now regarded as a key issue for victims and survivors of abuse in terms of building resistance to the negative impacts of domestic violence and other adverse experiences and developing a more empowered life. However, research in this area is a relatively new field (Ai and Park 2005), and the majority of the research on resilience to date has concentrated on children, rather than adults. Thus, concepts of resilience may need to be redefined and expanded for adults struggling with childhood domestic abuse and maltreatment experiences.

It has been suggested by some scholars that the research so far tends to obscure how individuals themselves experience their own resilience and the personal strengths which have led to their survival (see for example Anderson and Danis 2007). These strengths may be context-specific, may vary across different cultural and ethnic groups of people, or may be individually unique. They may not be recognised or acknowledged by others. Thus, adaptive and personally helpful facets of individual adult experiences, and ways of being resilient, may be ignored, distorted or misinterpreted, according to some previous studies, and may not fit into wider orthodoxies about what resilience is and what it is not (see, for example, Dietz 2000). Informants for this book talked about how their own strategies of resistance and resilience were often overlooked by colleagues and friends, and even themselves, so that they were regarded as less capable and more 'tragic', as the poet, 'Shaila' (above), puts it, than was often, in fact, the case.

Perhaps, then, the ways that adults manage and interpret difficulties and cope with earlier complex and often deeply personal childhood experiences of domestic abuse and other adversities are not yet well understood. For example, in the poem by 'Kate' in Chapter 1, she explores both how being fragile could be beneficial and creative on occasion, rather than 'pathetic', and also how the injustice of being criticised for sensitivity and emotionality – for not being resilient *enough* – could be damaging and re-victimising. She suggests that 'fragile is also human and to be treasured'. Being supposedly well-balanced, rather than sensitive and emotional, may, in reality, lead to emotional repression and shallowness, and may indeed be the opposite of a fulfilled life on occasion, as suggested in the following poem by an adult survivor of domestic abuse in childhood.

THE WELL-BALANCED PEOPLE
Still, I hear them,
the well-balanced people,
talking, joking away,

caught within their frameworks.
They are easy to feel sorry for.
I've tried to shut them out.

No time at all for superficial chatter.
Like boomerangs,
the lightness

shoots around me,
shining in the eyes like fireworks.
I am mesmerised,

yet always interrupted.
My barricades, you see,
are badly built.

And, still, I hear them,
the well-balanced people.
They graze my surfaces.

I must take care.
Or they will glue up my journeying,
hold me down and back,

and stop me flying, soaring…

The point here is that emotionality and sensitive unconventionality does not have to be a sign of weakness, but rather can be empowering in itself. Thus, resilience can be understood as the development of strategies of resistance to the abuse, but this can be the case even where these strategies are not the conventionally understood ones (Anderson 2001).

Anderson and Danis (2007) have presented a study of adult daughters of women who had experienced domestic violence. In their study, they found that the daughters were able to work out intensely personal strategies for emotional safety. The research identified routes to recovery which included developing personally significant ways to oppose, and to interrupt, the sense of powerlessness which tends to come with abuse. Where this had not been possible, the study participants gave examples of, at least, becoming able to 'withstand' this sense of powerlessness, even if they could not actively change it. The development of such techniques 'just for enduring it' had been adaptive and helpful for the adult daughters in terms of protecting themselves from feeling overwhelmed. Thus, 'withstanding' was identified as a strength in itself which the women could manage some of the time anyway, even while at other times feeling totally weak, anxious and powerless. Such an understanding may be useful to some survivors of domestic abuse in childhood.

Thus, building on one's own strengths and individual ways of coping, even if these are not recognised as such by others, may be the best way forward. In an American context, Banyard and Williams (2007) have conducted a multi-method study highlighting women's voices on recovery from abuse. This was a fascinating prospective study (see also Williams 1994) with girls interviewed in 1973–5, and then as grown women in 1990 (by then, aged 20–31 years) and 1997 (by then, aged 27–38 years) to assess changes in resilience as adults. The abuse in question in this study was child sexual abuse, rather than childhood domestic violence. However, the techniques the women identified that helped them may have some relevance to the latter, and were changing and complex.

Early resilience in childhood was associated with more positive and active later coping strategies as adults, but even where this was not the case and also where the women had experienced further abuse after growing up, change and positive outcomes were still possible. The study confirmed some previous work on adults (rather than solely on children) in understanding resilience as a dynamic process, not constant or consistent, but rather continually changing with circumstances (Banyard and Williams 2007; Luthar, Cicchetti and Becker 2000). Harvey (1996), for example, identified resilience as including various variable stages, with people moving backwards and forwards between them with the passage of time. Thus, resilience and recovery were ongoing, but not linear. Positive adaptations have been found to be helpful, but may interact with the trauma experienced in complex ways, so simplistic judgements about recovery are to be avoided (Glantz and Johnson 1999; Luthar *et al.* 2000).

For respondents in the Banyard and Williams (2007) study, recovery was an unfolding process, anticipated to extend across the lifespan in some cases. The participants identified the importance of 'second chances' after possible failure. They also identified 'turning points', and their critical importance and positivity in the recovery process. These significant turning points varied for individuals, and usually then led to personal growth and new understandings, in contrast to the victim remaining stuck in old, or negative, ways of thinking, as had previously been the case. For some of the women interviewed, progress and change towards more positive life functioning of this type could be clearly perceived, despite an initially discouraging prognosis.

These findings may give succour to those struggling to recover from domestic violence experiences in childhood. Even when things seem unremittingly bleak, there are possibilities for change and positivity. Overall, then, resilience, recovery and resistance to abuse are complex and changing, and may be individually specific. Typologies as to what counts as resilience do not work. These arguments have been briefly presented to indicate that simplistic reactions and narrow understandings of resilience are not appropriate when dealing with something as difficult, and individually specific, as recovering from childhood domestic violence.

General issues to be addressed and the lack of services doing so

The informants for this book from the focus group, testimonies, interviews and poems identified a range of difficulties that adults with childhoods affected by domestic abuse tend to experience, sometimes varying of course both by the gender of the person and also for families and individuals from minority communities. These difficulties, which therapeutic and agency responses need to take on, are discussed in detail in Chapter 4. To recap, among a wide range, they include:

• feeling a failure and always 'lesser' or in the wrong

• self-disgust, self-criticism and lack of confidence, self-worth and self-esteem

- depression, dejection, anxiety and mental health difficulties

- fear of conflict

- sleep disturbances

- difficulty with close or sexual relationships, with attachment issues and with personal boundaries, leading sometimes to revictimisation

- always feeling responsible and needing to take care of everything.

Many adults with abuse experiences, both women and men, including our respondents and testimony-givers, received the most support from family and friends. However, help may also be needed from agencies and professionals. Responses to the above difficulties, and interventions or counselling, delivered by helping agencies, with individuals who carry memories and emotional scars from childhood domestic violence, could ideally, in general, include:

- the promotion of adaptive and effective ways of coping with the maltreatment and adversity, individually tailored

- the enhancement of well-being and a sense of self-worth

- the prevention of revictimisation

- the nurturing of improvements in personal relationships

- the development of realistic personal boundaries

- the enabling of a happier, more fulfilled personal life.

However, to achieve such positive changes is difficult – possibly the work of a lifetime. The task for individuals is made even more difficult in that there are, in reality, as noted earlier, very few services and professional responses in the UK which take on these issues for adult survivors of domestic violence as children. Counselling, psychotherapy and other 'talking' therapies are the most likely to be of help, but are usually unavailable within social and welfare services. They can be accessed within the private (or sometimes community) sector, but can then become expensive. Statutory children's and family services are rarely of help unless the adult concerned has children, and, even then, interventions are likely to concentrate on the children and on parenting issues. Other services and agencies scarcely consider the matter or take it seriously.

Even internally, within agency staff and professional circles, childhood domestic abuse is frequently ignored and overlooked. Many adults with domestic violence experiences when they were children actually work in such services, but commonly they remain silent about these experiences. A book on raising the voices of survivors of domestic violence, called *Is Anyone Listening?*, identified this as a hidden issue within all types of helping services and particularly within domestic violence organisations (Hague *et al.* 2003). Survivors of abuse have always worked within domestic violence and refuge services, since the beginning, due to their commitment to the issue, and in order to 'give back' and to do what they can to assist others. The *Is Anyone Listening?* book paid tribute to professionals who had themselves experienced domestic abuse, stating that:

> Many have not felt able to be open about their status as survivors, reinforcing the point that women continue to be silenced about their experiences of domestic violence and that they may be regarded negatively... It is time to acknowledge and value their contribution, as part of increasing our willingness to respect and listen to survivors of domestic violence. Professionals in this situation have worked tirelessly on behalf of other abused women over many years and service provision has been transformed by their dedicated contributions. (Hague *et al.* 2003, p.147)

Domestic violence services

In general, the domestic violence sector may provide the services best able to address the relevant emotional issues for those who have experienced domestic abuse as children. Thus, adults in this situation may wish to approach these agencies for help. However, domestic violence services tend mainly to work with adults experiencing domestic abuse in their actual adult relationships, and with the children associated with these adults. They may have little time or expertise to address childhood issues carried forward from the past. Without re-entering the controversy of the inter-generational transmission of domestic violence discussed in Chapter 3, it is self-evident that some adult users of domestic violence organisations who have experienced abuse in their adult relationships will also have had abusive childhood experiences. Thus, these specialist organisations can, sometimes, be of help to such women through their provision of support, advocacy and both informal and formal counselling. Further extrapolating these important domestic violence services more generally to those addressing childhood (as well as adult) issues would be a step in the right direction. A clear suggestion arising from this book is that the sector should do so.

The development of (at least the beginning of) focused support services for adults in this situation, could usefully go hand-in-hand with further training and support for workers and volunteers, to deal with domestic violence issues carried on from childhood. It may be difficult to develop such services and approaches within current circumscribed funding regimes, cutbacks and the present hostile financial climate. Nevertheless, their increased provision and availability is clearly to be encouraged, through the further development and funding of the Women's Aid *Survivor's Forum* and through the extension of present domestic violence support provision, and of the counselling, outreach and empowering approaches they already use with survivors (Women's Aid 2011b).

'Anna' in her testimony in the previous chapter highlights the important role of the *Survivor's Handbook* and the *Survivor's Forum* and *Message Board*, and also of interactive social media networks. She also identifies the importance of programmes like the *Freedom Programme*, an empowering training and capacity-building programme for survivors of domestic violence, and the *Power to Change* guide for groups of domestic violence survivors produced by Women's Aid. Further developments of this type within the third (community) sector and within specific domestic violence services in the future, to assist those struggling with having experienced domestic abuse as children, are to be strongly recommended.

Feminist advocacy and counselling

Adult women with childhood experiences of domestic violence may benefit from feminist-type advocacy and counselling. Women's Aid and other domestic violence services usually use such understandings of the abuse of women by men, within a context of an awareness of gender inequality (Dobash and Dobash 1992; Hague and Malos 2005). It has been suggested by various scholars and commentators that ignoring these wider gender and power issues when conducting domestic violence work may hold back a person's recovery. For example, the Anderson and Danis (2007) study on adult daughters who experienced domestic abuse as children, noted above, found that, while resilience can be increased where there is general attention (personally and by support agencies) to self-esteem issues and to the development of mechanisms of social support, what is important is that it is the case that minimal attention is often paid by agencies conducting this work to exactly how resilience is forged in particular gendered circumstances for women.

These authors suggest that the actual dynamics of abuse by men, and of women's inequality and oppression within such relationships, and more widely in society, tend not to be addressed in either therapeutic responses or research on resilience factors (Anderson and Danis 2007). In contrast, their study suggests, therefore, that more attention needs to be paid – in supporting interventions and practice with adult survivors (both women and men) and also in the research agenda – to the gendered dynamics of domestic abuse and the oppressive environment created by the original abuser's actions. Features of trying, as a child, to live in such an oppressive environment were also identified and elaborated in practical lived terms in the testimonies in this book of 'Rose Wood' and 'Anna'. Dietz (2000) similarly discusses how work with adult survivors needs to recognise the intermeshed issues of oppression and abuse, and presents feminist challenges to the standard practice of clinical psychotherapy and social work. Building on the insights of Dietz and others, Anderson and Danis (2007) suggest (using the American term, 'batterers', not used in the UK) that:

> By recognizing the oppressive environment that was created by the batterers' abuse and the various ways in which they personally challenged that oppression, women may be able to transcend interpersonal notions of violence and develop a more comprehensive understanding within a feminist framework. (Anderson and Danis 2007, p.430)

A helpful development in the United States has been the formulation of a response to domestic abuse called 'feminist relational advocacy'. Developed by Lisa Goodman and others (see Goodman *et al.* 2009; also Goodman and Epstein 2008), feminist relational advocacy presents a new model informed by feminist and multicultural perspectives and theories of community psychology. This model presents a type of counselling which builds on the insights of the domestic violence movement, and on understandings of domestic violence and the abuse of women which are based on gendered power and control issues in relationships between men and women. Feminist relational advocacy has been found to be an effective response to the difficulties presented by low-income women experiencing depression in a recent evaluation study (Goodman *et al.* 2009).

Women's voices form a founding basis of this new model of counselling. Feminist relational advocacy is suggested (in the context of the USA but, surely, elsewhere also) to have a helpful future as a new tool for psychologists, counsellors and advocates. It uses concepts from women-defined and citizen advocacy, including: a) building mutually on the advocacy relationship between advocates/counsellors and service users; b) recognising that instrumental, practical support is inextricably intertwined with emotional support for most abuse survivors; c) valuing the women's narratives; and d) attention to external forms of oppression and not just to individual, internal and more traditionally 'therapeutic' concerns (Goodman *et al.* 2009). The method attempts to avoid pathologising the women concerned and evolves from the wealth of feminist theories, practice and understandings that have been developed over the last 30 years. It builds on the types of counselling conducted since the 1970s in refuge organisations, and aims to professionalise, validate and 'codify' these methods, incorporating a broad, political concept of male abuse and gender inequality. Feminist relational advocacy can clearly be useful to adult women who have experienced domestic abuse as children.

Getting help: what our informants recommended
The first issue
While some of the above discussions apply mainly to women victims only, they may also have resonance for men who witnessed domestic violence as young boys, especially those who identified strongly with their mothers. For both women and men, we turn now to specific helping techniques, personal steps and insights which may assist those wishing to address childhood experiences of domestic violence and to reach some sort of personal resolution. Clearly, taking such steps is not necessary or appropriate for everyone, and the dynamics of what happens in addressing these experiences will take as many different forms as there are victims. Perhaps the first, and in many ways the most important, development that needs to happen is for the person concerned to recognise, and accept, that they may need support or help, as most of our respondents suggested. 'Just try it. Don't just sit there and do nothing. That's what I'd say to them, if you asked me. To see if you can do something to make it better.' (Focus group member). If such a step seems too large, there needs to be, at least, a beginning commitment for the person to start to do their own emotional work on the issues, to begin what can seem like a very arduous, personal

journey. Without such a personal decision and undertaking, little is likely to change.

However, it can take many years to reach this point and to find the strength and confidence to decide that you need to address the impacts or to go out and seek help. One part of reaching such a point, according to our respondents, can be having to overcome feelings of shame and failure, first for seemingly 'not coping', and second for then having to ask for and receive help. Having to conceal, as a child, domestic violence experiences from everyone (as is often the case) may give rise to secrecy, a tendency to lie about difficult issues, and fear of exposure. Such a childhood may make it particularly hard to be open about experiences as an adult. All this may be complicated by the fact that the person may love, or have loved, the abuser, who is likely to have been their father or father-substitute. Our testimony-givers talk of how deeply they loved the perpetrator of the violence, in the context, also, of hating him and the abuse and the pain.

Thus, the process of addressing these issues is complicated and likely to be lengthy. Survivors of childhood domestic violence using this book may find it helpful to recognise how long it may take before they might feel it is possible to seek outside assistance. Hence, they may perhaps be able to gain some succour if they have not yet been able to do so, or have begun the process and then retreated from the task. Such starts and retreats may happen on many occasions. Time is needed, and there is no one right way forward. However, managing to overcome the initial trepidation, talking to someone about it, and seeking some assistance is almost certainly going to end up being beneficial.

What might help?

Our informants for this book included the poets, focus group members, testimony-givers and others. They suggested, between them, a wide range of ways which can lead to recovery or, at least, to less painful outcomes. These are presented in the following list, summarised, for ease of use by both survivors of domestic abuse and the professionals who attempt to assist them, and followed by further brief discussion of the main points they raised.

Ideas to aid recovery, according to survivors in this book

TALKING AND COUNSELLING SOLUTIONS

- talking to someone and being listened to

- confiding in partners, parents, children, family or colleagues and friends

- not being judged

- not being told that you are making a fuss about nothing

- talking about the issues in depth, and confronting them with a sympathetic safe person, time and time again, as needed

- working on recovery with a dedicated professional

- getting help from domestic violence services, refuges and the Women's Aid *Survivor's Handbook, Survivor's Forum* and *Message Board*

- participating in the *Freedom Programme* and other empowering and self-help programmes of training and support for domestic violence survivors, including the *Power to Change* Women's Aid guide to running support groups together

- undertaking counselling (including counselling techniques inspired by feminists and the domestic violence services)

- undertaking psychotherapy or making use of other therapeutic methods (which, preferably, also would include gendered understandings about domestic violence and violence against women); these could include relationship and sex therapy, if these prove helpful

- meeting up with others in the same situation, and sharing information, insights and experiences

- attending self-help or support groups

- participating in specific group work programmes with other adults who experienced domestic abuse as children

- using these meetings or group experiences to compare notes on what helped and what did not, and to assist each other to recover

- being referred to mental health support services, as needed

- being proactive in seeking assistance, 'not letting it go on and on without getting help' (focus group member).

PERSONAL DISCOVERIES, REALISATIONS AND WAYS FORWARD

- understanding and recognising the effects that your experiences have had on you, rather than minimising, concealing or repressing them

- coming to recognise that you were not to blame

- coming to recognise that the negative ways you might sometimes behave have an explanation

- coming to recognise that the 'symptoms' you have are shared by many others

- learning to like yourself and to develop self-respect

- coming to understand the dynamics of violence against women and domestic violence, and their impacts on children

- using visualisations to 'let go' of the feelings, of the memories – or even of images of the person (for example the empty chair technique, as discussed later)

- 'It might heal if you hang on in there and let lots of time pass' (focus group member)

- being vigilant about impacts on your children and making sure they are not affected

- being vigilant about setbacks, but accepting them if they occur

- having techniques to use when setbacks occur, but avoiding self-recrimination if you are not able to use them

- also avoiding self-recrimination if you are unable to recover or if you continue to experience negative emotional impacts

- developing inner resilience and a feeling of being able to cope and to be happy.

WRITING, CREATING AND TELLING OTHERS YOUR STORY

- writing poetry

- writing stories and journals

- possibly sharing and publishing these

- participating in radio broadcasts, speak-outs, survivor events, conferences, plays, etc.

- creating art to represent both the abuse and recovery

- possibly participating, similarly, in art events or exhibitions (sometimes specifically of survivors' art, etc.).

Moving away, leaving or returning

- moving away from the location where the abuse originally happened

- leaving the country and starting a new life elsewhere as an immigrant

- conversely, for some, moving back to where the experiences happened to confront and understand the past and their personal history.

Social, community and political engagement

- social engagement in community activities

- engaging in political and women's activism

- working on domestic abuse as a volunteer, manager or employee, and 'giving back' to refuges and domestic violence services and survivors

- experiencing wider social support from family and/or extended family members, for example grandparents, especially grandmothers, sisters, mothers, brothers, in-laws, children and other relatives and community members.

Education and employment

- gaining inspiration from teachers, social workers and other kind and helping professionals, as both a child and an adult

- undertaking further education and getting qualifications

- employment and having a successful or worthwhile job.

Loving relationships

- finding a kind and safe, supportive lover or sexual relationship

- the love and support of family and friends
- working on the issues together with your partner or lover.

THE ABUSER

- especially where the abuser had been a father or substitute father, being able perhaps to confront them or to talk through the issues
- similarly, personal resolution might be possible through interaction with the original victims of the domestic violence (mother or mother substitute usually)
- writing (and either sending, or not) letters to the abuser or to the adult who was abused
- perhaps being able to forgive the abuser, to 'let it all go'.

HEALING TECHNIQUES AND METHODS

- getting help from the doctor, the medical profession, or in some cases, alternative practitioners
- using medication to assist with sleep or depression
- using specific counselling and healing techniques (as discussed below)
- engaging in sport and exercise to release endorphins and good feelings
- yoga and other relaxation and meditation techniques, and incorporating these into daily life where possible
- stress reduction, going to stress management classes or engaging in personal stress-reducing techniques, and incorporating these into daily life where possible
- spirituality and religion
- seeing beautiful scenery, going to or living in the countryside
- growing gardens and plants
- bringing beautiful or happy experiences into your life in various ways
- finding inner peace, inner strength and self-balance.

Each item or quote in the list above could have its own sub-section. However, a brief selection of the major issues is presented here, as developed further in the next section.

Recovery and healing approaches

As the above list demonstrates, there are multiple ways in which childhood domestic violence experiences can be addressed, and victims can recover, or at least begin to do so. These issues apply to adult men attempting to address childhood experiences of domestic violence, as well as women, and to those from gay, lesbian and other minority communities or families of origin, although the existing research is mainly about women.

Various studies have identified how abused women are 'active learners in their own lives', trying to learn from their experiences as best they can (Hayes and Flannery 2000). In the Banyard and Williams (2007) research in the USA (discussed previously), adult abused women described precipitating or motivating factors which were almost exactly replicated in this book in the suggestions from the poets, the survivors in the focus group and those who gave testimonies and interviews. In trying to move towards recovery, what had helped the adults in this American study included a wide range of issues such as wanting the best for their children, spirituality (understood in its broadest sense to give personal succour), community engagement, and remembering the past rather than repressing it.

The 2007 Anderson and Danis study similarly found that strategies of resistance and coping (that arose originally for the adult daughters in their research as spontaneous reactions when they were children to the domestic abuse they had experienced) were honed in adulthood, developed in adult ways, and then used throughout their lives. The interviewees tried to make sense of their childhood experiences as best they could, and made attempts to understand their family histories as children in order to transcend them. They tried (not always successfully of course) to impose order on their previous chaotic or disordered experiences in their families of origin. As adults, keeping their own children, siblings and family safe was identified as of utmost importance (Anderson and Danis 2007).

Efforts to overcome previous childhood abuse, such as those made by the women in the above studies, may be small scale and personal, but deeply important for the individuals concerned. Recovery does not have to be a matter of grand therapy. Wade (1997) talks of 'small acts of living' or the 'everyday resistance to violence' to capture the non-dramatic but daily struggle towards recovering. Masten (2001) speaks of building resilience and resistance to abuse as 'ordinary magic'. Abuse survivors (including those with experiences of domestic abuse in childhood), both women and men, may indeed be able to weave such ordinary magic and can perhaps be considered as heroes of their own lives, as they struggle with the issue, just as were the children they used to be.

Safe spaces and sanctuaries

One of the ways in which the women in the Anderson and Danis study attempted recovery was by deliberately (or, sometimes, almost unconsciously) creating escapes or 'safe spaces' for themselves, physically, sexually or mentally (Anderson and Danis 2007; see, also, Anderson 2001). These spaces could be physical places to go to, especially if abuse was still occurring. Our own informants suggested, in this vein, the therapeutic personal value of finding a safe space, such as taking the dog for a walk, hot baths with a locked bathroom door, a special park, a private bedroom, and so on. Spaces could also be symbolic, or emotional in terms of creating safety or a place of sanctuary in the head and mind. Counsellors may be able to assist in the finding of such inner 'spaces'. The aim would be, deliberately and consciously, to develop an internal emotional or mental sanctuary to psychologically 'go to' in times of crisis, or in order to deal with childhood pain. Thus, either with or without a professional helper, it might be helpful for adults who lived with domestic violence as children first to identify, and then to deliberately use, visit or imagine themselves into such personal spaces as a deliberate strategy for coping.

Talking and counselling solutions

It is clear from the earlier discussions that talking to a trusted adviser, friend, family member or counsellor is probably the best way to address adverse childhood experiences such as domestic violence. All the testimonies and research studies attest to this. One of our focus group members spoke of:

> finally being able to talk about it, rather than pretending it was nothing. Accepting it properly if you like... Giving it its due. It is such a relief just to be open about it and then to get some help with dealing with it. It took me years really...

Breaking the silence, finding a confidante, possibly a sister, grandmother, relative or friend – or possibly the original person who experienced the domestic abuse – and talking it through together, can be liberating in the extreme. Friends, present partners and family can have the biggest part to play. But professional helpers and counsellors can also sometimes facilitate transforming experiences, as we discuss throughout the chapter. Domestic violence counsellors need special training to address the prevalence, impacts and gendered power dynamics of abuse, as also discussed earlier. At best, they may then be able to accompany the victim on the journey to becoming a resilient and transformed survivor.

Thus, with the help of family, support people or professionals, it is important for victims, both women and men, to identify and 'own' their childhood experiences. With such friendship or counselling support, survivors can come to recognise that they were not to blame for the abuse, but also that they might sometimes behave, as a result of their childhood domestic violence experiences, in negative ways which can then be understood and addressed. Family, friends and professionals can be helpful, also, in identifying and helping the person to 'own' the positive coping mechanisms which they will almost certainly have previously developed and which are likely to have led to resilience (even if not consistently so). Consciously locating these often previously semi-conscious or confused strategies, and further developing them, is almost bound to be of help, with the assistance of counsellors and therapists, if necessary.

Specific therapeutic and counselling are discussed in the sections on 'specific healing techniques and methods' and on 'Handbooks and guides' below. Domestic violence services may also use similar methods currently or be able to advise on where to access them.

Social, community and political engagement

All our informants talked of the importance of participating, where possible (which it might not always be), in group or community activities, activism around domestic violence or social engagement. Both 'Rose' and 'Anna' who gave their testimonies now work in domestic abuse or rape support services, for example, and have found this involvement to be therapeutic and cathartic. Similarly, 'Patrick' who contributed the testimony in the next chapter has dedicated most of his adult professonal life to working with, and raising the voices of, children in care both practically and in terms of policy and writing. All the research confirms this finding in terms of the importance of socially engaging work and of external support and social networks, as, for example, strongly identified in the Banyard and Williams (2007) research. Abuse victims in this and other studies were able to achieve some aspects of protection and of a sense of competence and control through connections with others (Banyard and Williams 2007; Hobfoll 2002).

Community groups for adults with painful pasts of domestic abuse and for their own children, together or separately, and actual conjoint therapy for mothers and children together have also been found to be beneficial (for example, Sullivan, Egan and Gooch 2004), as noted in Chapter 6. Thus, interacting with others, gaining support, sharing experiences, and engaging in community and social activity and activism, have been found, almost universally, to be helpful. Just finding out that experiences and feelings are shared by many others can be healing in itself. It was indeed on such principles of women sharing together and helping each other to become stronger that the original domestic violence movement to establish refuges and support projects was built (Dobash and Dobash 1992; Hague and Malos 2005).

In the previously discussed Anderson and Danis (2007) study of adult daughters of abused women, the daughters built support networks for themselves with others whenever they could, and tried to find constructive activities outside the home (see, similarly, Mullender *et al.* 2002, in the context of children). In fact, in most studies, grown-up victims remembering domestically abusive childhoods tried, where they could, to get outside support, engaged in external activities and sought out other supportive and caring adults (see for example Humphreys 2001, in an article helpfully entitled 'Turnings and adaptations in resilient daughters of battered women'). Certainly, engaging in political, community or social activities can be useful, or even transformative, but may be too daunting for some – in which case it would be important to try something else without engaging in self-blame!

Writing, creating, art and telling others your story

It can be cathartic to write about the abuse experiences or to paint them. Our various informants spoke of poems, testimonies, journals, stories, plays – writing any of these could be healing in itself, even if the results were never witnessed by others. Similarly, painting or drawing about both the abuse and possible ways to overcome it can be useful in trauma recovery. It does not need to be important that such works of creation and catharsis are publicly exposed. However, where creative activities lead to public view, as in performed plays, anthologies of poems by survivors, survivor events or speak-outs, and art exhibitions (sometimes put on by domestic violence organisations), the therapeutic effect can be magnified. 'I did a painting, I had never done one before and they put it in the exhibition. Well! I was so proud. Really. It makes me feel tearful...'

All the poets and testimony-writers for this book stated that the process of contributing to the content and providing creative writing to be included and read by others had been healing.

Education and employment

Our informant 'Rose' specifically identified kind, concerned and reliable educators and teachers as having been vital in her own journey through childhood domestic abuse. The head teacher who read her stories, for example, had been transformative in her troubled childhood. Similarly, other survivors talked of particularly important social workers, teachers, refuge workers and other confidantes, in both childhood and adulthood, who had helped to break the silence and bring the issues into the open. 'Anna' spoke in her testimony of ongoing education, getting a good degree and transforming her life through educational achievement (even though she still wished she had done better, despite, in fact, doing very well). These have been key ingredients for her in moving on from her abusive childhood and bad memories. Others also identified getting a good job and professional satisfaction as ways forward.

Loving relationships

One of the best ways to recover can be through the love and support of a kind and understanding lover or partner. 'Rose' discussed the importance of loving relationships in her testimony and, subsequent to her traumatic childhood, has had a happy marriage for 30 years. Some informants had found solace in relationships with women which, they suggested, might be gentler and less tied in with gendered power issues. Building personal relationships and establishing appropriate personal and sexual boundaries can be particularly difficult, however, when trying to recover from childhood domestic violence, and may need ongoing care, sympathetic input, loving understanding, and forgiveness and tolerance on all sides.

Using stress-reducing and relaxation techniques

Our informants particularly identified the pursuit of inner calm and peacefulness as a way forward. This might include meditation, yoga, relaxation practice, stress management techniques, sport and visualisations. They suggested that the impact of such practices can be life enhancing, life transforming, and for some life saving, especially where they are integrated into daily life.

The abuser: challenge and resolution

As our informants point out in the list above, confronting, meeting with, resolving issues with – or forgiving – the perpetrator of domestic violence experiences in childhood, where safe to do so, can be a useful way forward. Especially where the abuser has been a father or substitute father, being able perhaps to talk it though rationally and clearly may help the move towards a personal resolution. Challenging the perpetrator, explaining the personal impact and ongoing ramifications of their actions, being angry with them perhaps: all these may be liberating, although the support of a trained counsellor or skilled and committed personal friend may be needed. Our informants pointed out that writing to the perpetrator is usually helpful in dealing with the issues, even if the letter is never sent. Again, working with a counsellor on the content and implications of the letter can be useful. It can similarly be helpful to attempt talking and resolution with the person who was abused, often a mother or mother substitute.

If the people concerned have died, visiting the graves if they exist, or other significant places, can be of benefit. Saying what needs to be said, or writing a letter to the dead person, are often constructive ways forward, even though they cannot hear the words and the letter cannot be sent. One of our informants spoke of sitting in the garden of remembrance where her father's ashes had been scattered and, after much hard emotional work and many visits, finally being able to forgive him and say she loved him. However, two of our testimony-givers had never seen their fathers again. Again, there is no one right way forward – although coming to a feeling of peace and resolution in regard to the original perpetrator is very likely to be the most healing outcome.

Along the way, the emotional challenges are many. Challenging, being angry with or resolving the past with the abuser are complex paths to take and demand strength, confidence and support. Such meetings, or memorialising, are almost certain to be painful and upsetting, but the outcomes can be an empowered and resolved future for those carrying the pain of witnessing domestic abuse in childhood.

Handbooks and guides

There are many handbooks and guidebooks now available to assist those wishing to recover from experiences of abuse and adversity as children, as well as the resiliency manuals noted in Chapter 6 (which can be drawn on to assist adults as well as children). In the UK, useful lists of such handbooks are published by the NSPCC and some other organisations. Victims of childhood domestic abuse may find these helpful, although few address the issue specifically, and the most common handbooks are about recovery from child sexual or physical abuse. The techniques used will have some resonance in the case of childhood domestic abuse also, but adults in this situation might feel awkward and sensitive about using such material, since their own experiences are likely to have been very different. Nevertheless, insights can be gained.

A good starting point is the ground-breaking book by Judith Herman, *Trauma and Recovery* (1997), originally published in 1992, and further work by Herman (for example Herman, Russell and Trochi 1986; Herman 1992). Her landmark book, on which much subsequent work on trauma recovery has drawn, builds on feminist perspectives on abuse and power. Herman develops deep and pioneering understandings of the recovery process after the experience of complex post-traumatic stress disorder due to child abuse, domestic violence, sexual assault, incest and political terror. This book has changed how both professionals and abuse victims deal with abusive experiences from childhood. Survivors of domestic violence as children may wish to consult it, together with subsequent contributions from Herman.

The book is not a step-by-step practical guide, but rather an overall treatment of recovery from trauma. It is suggested that adverse and abusive experiences often give rise to concealment and conflicting responses which attempt not only to hide the trauma, the guilty secret, but also to return to it again and again. Herman elaborates in detail how recovery is about empowerment which can be facilitated through developing healing therapeutic (and other) relationships, and then working on the stages of recovery. She suggests that these stages include establishing strategies for safety, reconstructing the traumatic story, using remembrancing and mourning the loss, and finally reconnection with the person's community.

Often using Herman's framework, many further resources now exist to deal with recovery from personal abuse and trauma. They frequently deal with identifying the impacts of abuse and then look at how to develop therapeutic relationships with professional helpers, including the gradual evolution of trust between the counsellor and the counsellee, a key issue in this type of sensitive and distressing work. Handbooks and guides also often discuss how to deal, practically and emotionally, with such issues as depression, self-harm, lack of boundaries, sexual difficulties, poor parenting, damaged personal relationships, and coping with fear and destructive memories (see for example Sanderson 2008). Various guides develop programmes of work for professionals to assist in victims' recovery, including recommending partnership or inter-agency joint working for helping organisations, and offering advice for professionals.

Many also present exercises and activities for individuals and groups to assist abuse victims overcome negative memories and feelings (Adamson 2003; McQueen et al. 2008). The latter book, *Psychoanalytic Psychotherapy after Child Abuse*, edited by Daniel McQueen, the late Cathy Itzin and others, and mentioned in Chapter 3, looks at the wide-ranging clinical evidence for the effectiveness of psychoanalytic and psychotherapeutic approaches to childhood neglect and abuse, including domestic violence. The edited collection reflects on these therapeutic approaches, from a broad spectrum of experience which includes survivor group perspectives, and which confirms that psychoanalytic psychotherapy provides (for some, not all, survivors, of course, and in appropriate circumstances) the framework for helpful journeys to recovery.

Thus, help, and even inspiration, can be found in the wealth of material now available, as can, perhaps, be illustrated in a few further examples. In *Healing the Trauma of Abuse*, Copeland and Harris (2000) present a practical step-by-step workbook to recovery from different types of abuse in childhood. They discuss, in several sections, empowerment of the victim, trauma recovery techniques, creating life changes, and finally closing the process, and they develop concepts of self-knowledge, self-management, readiness to change and choice for survivors. The authors look at physical and sexual boundaries, self-esteem, self-soothing (a helpful concept for abuse survivors of all types), and a variety of other techniques for healing and recovery, including caring for yourself in a healthy way, taking ownership of your own recovery, setting goals, and valuing your own unique coping methods.

In a further example (among many), Skogrand and colleagues (2007) from the University of Utah identify negative childhood experiences as a 'dark thread' running through the cloth of life (in their book, *Surviving and Transcending a Traumatic Childhood*, the resource for survivors noted in Chapter 3). The book weaves together 90 unique testimonies of how individuals were able to transcend this dark thread of abuse to build healthy, happy lives as adults. These rich testimonies emphasise the importance of accessing therapy and support groups, building supportive relationships with others, finding significant people who can provide help, and identifying survival strategies. Thus, this powerful research provides a self-study guide for developing a deeper understanding of the healing process. The stories demonstrate the considerable capacity of human beings to adapt and grow positively even after deeply damaging childhood experiences. Working with a handbook of this type can be an ideal step for those attempting to recover from their childhood memories and experiences of domestic violence.

Specific healing techniques and methods

Many specific counselling and therapeutic techniques exist, including, as noted, specific techniques for uncovering and addressing the power and other dynamics of domestic abuse, and enabling the survivor to learn about these. This short discussion is merely a pointer towards a few of the vast variety of further counselling approaches and methods that may be of help, and cannot claim to be a professional therapeutic coverage. However, it can be readily seen, even in a non-professional discussion of therapeutic techniques, that most therapies recognise that there are stages to recovery as well as oscillations, setbacks, turning points and a 'backwards and forwards' trajectory, as we have discussed. Therapeutic change can be shaky, irregular, unpredictable and jagged, and it is likely to be important for the counsellee to understand this. Within such an understanding, cognitive behavioural therapy, personal 'mindfulness' techniques, and solution-focused therapy can all be of help in different ways, and the stages to be emotionally negotiated in the change process may include pre-contemplation, contemplation, preparation, action and, finally, maintenance of positive development.

The techniques used may enable the person to learn how to regulate their emotions, to manage painful symptoms that cause suffering and distress, and to minimise their own unhelpful responses. The aim is likely to be to establish safety and stability in the person's life and relationships, to set goals and work out ways of building towards those goals, and to move through emotional stages of remembering, 'owning', grieving and resolving.

A whole realm of such techniques exist which can be drawn upon. The long-term aim is often to facilitate the person coming to respect and even 'love' themselves and to resolve their painful and traumatic pasts. Investigations with the counsellor can move into the realms of psychotherapy, art therapy, making and working with personal journals, workbooks and histories, and learning to experience anger and how to get past the memories and negative impacts to create a new life. They can also have more practical outcomes in terms of enabling entry into support groups, further education or jobs, Techniques may include addressing powerlessness, shame, rage, guilt and distrust and the performance of re-enactments of what happened in the past and of both the positive or, if relevant, abusive patterns in current relationships. Being able to establish healthy personal, emotional and sexual boundaries may be the specific subjects of some therapies, as may creating mental or emotional sanctuaries. Relationship counselling, parenting classes, couple counselling and individual therapy, including sex therapy for some, may have a part to play in enabling the survivor of childhood domestic abuse to build healthy and happy relationships in adulthood.

Clearly, most therapeutic interventions affirm that recovery is a process, that it may be a long one, as noted throughout this chapter, and that a key issue is that survivors need to be able to pace themselves (see Copeland and Harris 2000). Thus, it is important to stay with the process (more or less, and to varying degrees at different times, perhaps) for the duration. However, it can also be important to take breaks. Some therapists, for example, speak of 'banana split' therapies in which people are encouraged to sometimes deliberately stop any attempts to address their painful pasts, to give themselves permission to go out and to have fun (Howes 2010).

Most counselling techniques challenge the often expressed idea that an individual with traumatic childhood experiences may be 'too broken' to ever really heal. Survivors have sometimes been characterised as having 'broken hearts' (Howes 2010), which seem to keep on getting broken and re-broken, but therapeutic work may enable the broken heart to begin to heal. Very specific counselling techniques can be of help. A classic is the 'empty chair' technique, one of a variety of interactive techniques derived from gestalt therapy. This technique has various versions. It has sometimes been critiqued as being potentially damaging and, thus, is best used in partnership with a skilled therapist, in which case the relationship between the client and therapist needs to be part of the therapy. Many across the world have benefited from 'empty chair' counselling. Survivors address their feelings and thoughts about the person who committed abuse in their lives to the empty chair (which may be a real chair or a metaphorical one). In variations of the method, they may then act out an imagined reply from the person concerned (who had committed the original domestic violence) while seated on the chair themselves. Alternatively, the therapist may take such a role, sitting on the chair and acting the part of the abuser (although within therapeutic ethics and working principles and with carefully controlled aims). Survivors of childhood domestic abuse may find such techniques particularly useful.

Other therapeutic techniques include classic approaches such as 'voice dialogue' which includes analysis of the multiple 'selves' that may make up a person, some of which may have resulted from childhood abuse experiences. These particular selves may be damaged, and then may be 'disowned' by the individual concerned, whereas other selves will be undamaged. Positive change may be able to be achieved by interaction between these 'selves' with the help of a voice dialogue therapist (from the vast literature available, see, for example, the work of the famed pioneers of this approach, Hal Stone and Sidra Stone 1993a; 1993b).

Such techniques may revolve around attempting to heal 'the inner child' who was damaged by adverse events in childhood and a host of 'inner child' therapies can be accessed to assist emotional healing work. Further, in terms of personal resolution, visualisation techniques can be useful in addressing issues, perhaps, for example, to assist in 'letting go' of attachment to the perpetrator in a visual way. For example, the perpetrator can be visualised in the 'mind's eye' on a stage, or framed in a picture, and then be visualised disappearing slowly and peacefully into the distance or the past, or becoming smaller and smaller and less threatening. Alternatively, they could be visualised apologising, being forgiven by, and embracing the visualiser. The first author has used these techniques successfully with individuals, with empowering and enriching results. Thus, visualisation can be a key part of laying the feelings and the past to rest, resolving them, or making one's peace. Some of our testimony-givers suggest that making one's peace in this way is an essential part of healing.

Thus, in conclusion, for both victims of childhood domestic violence experiences and for professionals working with them, some of the approaches and methods noted in this chapter may be useful. For victims, though, the most important issue may just be to take the plunge and to start the process of talking to someone, getting help or addressing self-recovery. The possibilities for rediscovering, or for creating, a happy future are multiple, and can perhaps be inspiring, even if difficult and sometimes conflicted. This book strongly encourages adults struggling with the painful impacts of experiencing domestic abuse as children to give it a try. One could say, nothing ventured, nothing gained.

Chapter 9

Both Pain and Being Shielded

Testimony of 'Patrick'

I came from a working-class family of the 1950s, and grew up in the North of England. My mother was Lancastrian and my father Irish and they had three sons. We lived as part of the Irish Diaspora in the Manchester cotton towns. I was the middle of the three brothers, so, in childhood, I think I was considerably protected. In fact, it was much later, only fully in adulthood when I talked with my elder brother at length, that I began to fully realise and understand the extent to which I had probably been protected by both him and my mother from full knowledge of the domestic violence that she was experiencing from my father. Therefore, there is an important sense in which I was not as badly affected as my older brother.

Through most of my early childhood, my father 'worked away' in construction work. I later learned that this was what was often referred to as an 'Irish divorce', the point being that culture and religion in the 1950s made divorce and separation for Catholics very difficult. (My mother, though not born Catholic, 'converted' in order to marry my father in a Catholic church.)

When my father worked away, he returned relatively often for weekends and holidays, and it was at such times that the potential for arguments occurred, which might culminate in potential or actual violence. I feel it should be said that alcohol (possibly even alcoholism) was a factor. Certainly, my father was a heavy drinker and my mother, for sure, 'liked a drink'. Hence, the incidents were far more likely to happen after closing time and certainly after my bedtime. While I recognise that alcohol does not cause domestic violence in itself, it certainly made it much worse in our household.

Perhaps the combination of the protection and shielding provided by my brother and my mother, together with the fact that, since my father was often away, the incidents were spread apart, were factors that made a difference about the level of the impact which they had upon me. Later, when I was in my teens, my mother and father began to live together full-time again, and together ran the local Irish Democratic League Club. Whatever its historical origins, this had become, by the early 1960s, an Irish drinking and social club. Needless to say, this did not alleviate problems with alcohol in the family. So, there was a period where incidents of arguments, shouting, fear, anxiety and potential or actual violence were more frequent.

I do remember an occasion of physically trying to protect my mother when I was perhaps 15. I think I was successful, but I do not have an absolute accurate recollection. I also remember my mother crying and being filled with fear and anxiety on various occasions. I think the violence was not as bad as in some families I knew, though that is not to excuse it. I saw her physically injured one time with a black eye which was very upsetting, but I never otherwise saw her actually hurt.

By the age of 15 or 16, there was a sense in which I was able now to protect myself by simply doing all the interesting and exciting things newly available to me as an adolescent in the early 1960s. Though the events clearly distressed me, and obviously distressed my mother, they seemed to always have been stopped by the morning when everyone was sober again.

My relationship with my father was very ambiguous. While abhorring his terrible temper and abusive behaviour, I greatly enjoyed the company and attention proffered to me by him and by the many Irish working-class men and women who would often visit the house or whom I would see at the Club. They would make a big fuss of me and make me feel important, and were always good for a shilling or two, especially if they were tipsy! One of the things that made it ambiguous for me is the whole identity issue for Diasporic Irish people. I have since embraced this identity more clearly and I now hold Irish citizenship.

I feel sure that the experience of my family coloured very much my own approach to a long-term partnership and to having children. For example, in the climate of 1970s feminism, it might have been possible for me to have fathered a child but, by consent, not necessarily to have been a hands-on parent, as many men were at the time. I would have found this very difficult to bear because I would have seen myself as an absent or irresponsible parent like my father had sometimes been. This made me want to be (and, in fact, be, I hope) a better and more responsible parent.

It was clear that the separations were to do with the arguments, the anger and the violence. It was also clear that the incidents of anger and violence frightened, damaged, hurt and upset my mother, and this of course reinforced my attitude about the inappropriateness and damaging nature of domestic violence since it diminishes all concerned: men, women and children. I guess it also made me more able to understand and embrace, as far as a man can embrace, the emerging feminist movement of that time, and especially the part of that movement which challenged, and challenges, domestic violence.

Though I feel that my background caused me pain and caused my older brother even more pain, I still would not wish to have been born into any other family and I certainly would not have wished to have been taken away from my family because I had been 'harmed by witnessing domestic violence', as sometimes now happens, though of course I may have been so harmed. Despite the harm I probably did experience, I can only say that I appreciate the Irish Diasporic identify and memories that were provided by my father, albeit through an accident of birth. At least he gave me that.

By the same token, I spent much of my adult personal and working life supporting people and activists in the domestic violence field and feel that my experience in my family paradoxically has stood me in good stead, though of course I would not have chosen it. (For paid work, I have worked for many years in social work, children's rights and child protection.)

My experiences of domestic abuse clearly upset me. I didn't like it and I tried to stop it when I could. However, in working-class, low-income Irish Lancastrian families, there tended at the time to be a 'don't worry, keep going' ethos because, in all honesty, there were so many negative and unjust and upsetting life situations that one could worry about, but there were not the resources to do anything about them. So, in a sense, the 'don't worry' ethos was a necessary survival technique. However, it is also true that it can be used to shield oneself from pain and difficulty when it might be better to confront and deal with them. However, as a child, and even as an adolescent, I suspect that I found it easier 'not to worry' than to confront something that, in the main, I was powerless to prevent, though of course I do remember physically intervening on some occasions and being emotionally upset about what was taking place.

I would like to add that there is almost inevitably for children and young people the difficulty that they often love, and of course depend upon, both parents, and this also inevitably leads to conflicting emotions, confusion and insecurity where there are the sort of experiences in the family that I outlined above.

There is a difference between myself and my brother. As I have said, I was greatly protected by him, and I strongly suspect he directly collaborated with my mother to shield and protect me from what was taking place, and also to plan with her how to deal with my father and with the domestic violence. He was badly affected in that, because of the responsibility that he took when he was a young teenager or that was inappropriately thrust upon him, he carried anger and deep distress and acute pain about the situation to his deathbed. He protected our mother, too, as best he could. What he was always trying to do, as a faithful son, was his best for his mother.

My other brother was much, much younger than us and was affected by the arguing and violence, but less so. In fact our mother tragically died of cancer when he was only 14, a catastrophic trauma for such a young person, and for us all.

It is a profound regret to me that my older brother and I were only able to discuss the family traumas and our father's violence to our mother in our later life, effectively when he had himself become terminally ill. If I am less scathed, by which I mean less anguished, damaged and angry than my brother was about the situation, it is clearly because of the protection afforded to me by him and, of course, by my mother. I would like to dedicate this short account with deep gratitude, to them both posthumously. They gave me the great gift of protection and the possibility of a relatively happy and unscarred childhood.

Chapter 10

It Can Be Over

Conclusions

This book has attempted to break new ground in regard to people who have had domestic violence experiences as children. The adult impacts, anguish and emotional scarring resulting from such childhood experiences have rarely attracted much in the way of attention before, except from some therapists and domestic violence services. We have attempted in this book to begin to fill the gap.

There is little material on which to draw. The outcomes for adults of living with, or witnessing, domestic abuse in childhood is an under-researched area, particularly in the UK, where little robust research evidence exists to assist policy-makers, counsellors, domestic violence workers and other practitioners. There is more in North America, which we have explored in this book in order to inform professionals, and to provide as much information on the issue as possible. Thus, the book is part of breaking the silence which tends to surround the issue. No one seems to take it very seriously. In the past, at least, it has been just accepted as a 'fact of life'. But for those who experience domestic violence between their parents or parent substitutes as children, it can be a devastating and painful adult road to travel.

In terms of breaking the silence, we have tried also both to raise the profile of adults who were exposed to domestic abuse as children, and to raise the profile of the issue for professionals in the field. Our aim has been to contribute to the process of getting the issue taken seriously, of persuading helping agencies that they should take it on board, and of providing some guidance and ideas for how survivors of childhood domestic violence can recover. Breaking silences, enabling previously ignored issues to be taken seriously and increasing their invisibility: these can be arduous tasks, however, and are often prone to setbacks, as well as to inspiration and new approaches. Our hope is that we have at least made a beginning.

Both children and the adults they later become can manage to cope with domestic violence and to avoid negative emotional impacts, and many do. But it is also the case that many do not and, instead, carry pain and emotional impacts throughout life. In the book, we have discussed the outcomes for adults resulting from domestic abuse experiences in childhood, in terms both of the available research and of the moving and sometimes brave testimonies, insights and words of survivors. Drawing on commissioned and specially written poems, on interviews, on the focus group and on the personal written testimonies themselves, we have attempted to meld together the voices of survivors and what the research tells us. The impacts for both men and women can include feeling a failure and always in the wrong, but simultaneously feeling responsible for everything and everyone. They can include lack of confidence and self-worth, depression, self-hatred, self-criticism, dejection, anxiety, mental health difficulties, suicidal impulses and suicide, fear of conflict, sleep disturbances and difficulty with close or sexual relationships. Our informants related a devastating catalogue of such impacts for adults. They also explained how these painful personal impacts are very often hidden by the person concerned, often disguised – and then, to make it even worse, overlooked and ignored in general in the world at large. Scarring, rejection and concealed pain fill this life territory.

We have also looked at the impacts on children of domestic violence in order to perhaps provide some pointers to how to address the issue before the adult scarring and damage has occurred. We have described helpful responses and practical ways to help with healing and recovery for adults and also for children. For both, the research points out that responses by helping agencies and professionals need to take on board a range of diversity issues (at different levels and in a variety of ways, of course, for children, for women or for men). These include the important power dynamics of domestic violence, as well as equality issues including gender, ethnicity, cultural and class background, poverty and deprivation, sexuality, disability and other relevant issues.

For children, responses can include direct therapeutic or social work interventions, children's specialised services within the domestic violence sector, working with children's resilience, group work and specialised techniques (such as the 'jug of loving water', as one example). Within all of these approaches, we present research and practical evidence of how important it is that helping agencies forefront children's views and voices in designing their responses. All attempts at help need to be led by the child.

For adults, both women and men, we present a range of ways in which agencies and professionals can be of help, as well as ideas and suggestions for possible healing that survivors themselves may wish to use directly. These include building resilience as adults; but it is clear, from the survivors' testimonies and painful words, that the ways in which adults demonstrate resilience and coping in regard to childhood domestic violence are not always well understood. Survivors might be heroes of their own lives but this might not be recognised by anyone else.

Ways to heal and helping techniques need to place the views of the people concerned centre-stage, and to be validating and empowering. They include enabling the domestic violence sector to expand their services to take on the issue, and facilitating survivors themselves to engage in confidence-building community and social involvement, education and employment possibilities. Recovery and support work of all types highlights the importance of talking to someone, rather than holding it all inside alone. Taking the (sometimes very hard) step of seeking help from family, from friends and from professionals, including therapists and counsellors, is a key road forward.

Ways to deal with such painful experiences may well also encompass the use of visualisation and stress-reducing techniques, sport and physical activity, moving away from where the abuse happened (or, alternatively, going back to confront the past), getting peer support and help from others in the same situation, and addressing the previous violence directly with the abuser (safely and with support) or with the person originally abused. Counselling help (sometimes long-term) may draw on a wide range of therapeutic and psychological approaches. These may include addressing lack of self-worth and self-esteem, and dealing with depression, with possible lack of personal boundaries, and with relationship and sexual problems. In some cases, it may be necessary to address serious issues of mental health difficulties and suicidality. In these endeavours, as we have discussed throughout, learning about the gendered nature of domestic violence, why it happens, and who was responsible, are usually essential to enable growth and personal understanding.

A wide variety of specific ways to build strength and confidence and to resolve painful personal histories of childhood domestic violence have been presented, encompassing therapies like voice dialogue, feminist relational advocacy and inner child counselling, and also specific healing techniques (such as the 'empty chair' technique). Overall, what seems to be most often needed is talking – and then talking some more – with a counsellor, professional worker, helper or friend, and embarking together with supportive others on the personal journey to recovery and to leaving it behind.

What we have wanted to emphasise throughout this book, and in the inspiring testimonies from adult survivors, both in prose and poems, which provide its foundation, is that recovery is possible. Our hope is that the methods and therapies and personal ways forward that we have discussed may provide inspiration and ideas for recovery for those carrying scars from childhood and for their supporting professionals. It is clear that what is needed, in one way or another, is achieving personal resolution.

Thus, carrying the weight and pain does not have to be a life-long sentence. The ideas and discussions contained here may be able to bring some light to those damaged and hurt by domestic violence experiences as children, including those who have not felt able to talk about this hurt before to anyone at all, or to seek help and support. We trust you can be reassured that experiencing childhood domestic abuse *is* a real and often serious issue of abuse – but it *is* possible to resolve it.

In summary, then, the book has melded academic research discussions with the voices of survivors and creative material in the form of poems, interviews and personal testimonies with the aim of making it an enriching read. The hope of the authors is that it will assist survivors of childhood domestic violence and the professionals who work with them, that it will open new doors, and, perhaps for some, that it will enable personal transformations, resolutions and a happier future.

We finish with a poem by 'Susan' who specially wrote it for this book, movingly confirming our principal message that the pain for adults carried from childhood can come to an end. It is possible to recover. It is possible to leave it behind and to achieve personal fulfilment, free of hurtful anguished memories and pain. The poem starts with a carefree child, followed by internalised wretchedness, but ends in resolution and optimism, not only for the author, but for both her parents too. It was possible for them all to transform their lives. The final message of the poem, and of the book, is that it can be over. It can be over.

IT'S OVER (A POEM OF MEMORY)

[I]
If I close my eyes
And think about those days,
My childhood.
I remember those normal happy
Childhood
Days.

You know,
The ones that seem to always have shiny weather.

Playing,
Having adventures.
I often wonder when I first got to know.

I remember knowing, and then I never didn't know again.

But when was it?
Was I nine or maybe eleven?
Did the knowledge creep up on me?

Later it was always there.
I remember arguments and the sound of things
Crashing.
Occasional bandages.
A broken finger made into a joke.

Accusations that my mum
Bled too easily.
A doctor called by my dad, panicking.
I felt horrified and frightened.

I always thought I could fix it
But I never could.

I felt guilty and eaten up with it.
I tried to hide it all the time,
So no one else knew ever.

Not ever.
Even my closest friend.

I felt so inferior and scared
All the time.
Supposing they found out,
I couldn't have gone on.
It didn't seem to happen to anyone else,
Not that I knew anyway.

It was like a great tower of pain
Pressing in on me.
And I thought I was all alone with it
And so young and shy and vulnerable.

Of course
There were good times too.
It wasn't always bad.

In fact lots of the times were probably OK.
We'd go places, go for trips,
Play cards and games
All together often.

There are smiling photos.

But then there were times
When it was a nightmare.

I'd tell my mum to just give in and keep quiet,
But she wouldn't
(To her credit, I see now).

[II]
Later, when I was grown,
I left
And I would only see them separately,
On their own,
Without the arguing.

Without me wanting to scream at them.
And fighting back the rising panic and tears.

It was easier.

They did resolve it in the end.
They moved apart and it was better.

It was so much better that way.
They both got good new lives.
They were both happier.
I was too.

Because they were good people,
Wonderful people,
She was.

But, to be honest,
So was he
In all those other important ways.

Parents to be so proud of.
It was better then,
They could both grow
And feel proud of themselves
And strong.

And I was proud of them too,
So very proud.

Proud of both of them.
Not just my mum.

And,
After years,

I could finally let it go.

And it was all over.

It was finished
Over.

Life could be gold-coloured after all.

It is finished.

It is over.

References

Abrahams, C. (1994) *The Hidden Victims: Children and Domestic Violence.* London: NCH Action for Children.

Adamson, L. (2003) *The Ultimate Guide to Overcoming Sexual and Childhood Abuse.* Leybourne, Kent: Diviniti Publishing.

Afifi, T., Boman, J., Fleisher, W. and Sareen, J. (2009) 'The relationship between child abuse, parental divorce, and lifetime mental disorders and suicidality in a nationally representative adult sample.' *Child Abuse and Neglect 33*, 3, 139–47.

Ai, A. and Park, C. (2005) 'Possibilities of the positive following violence and trauma: Informing the coming decade of research.' *Journal of Interpersonal Violence 20*, 2, 242–50.

Anda, R., Felitti, V., Brown, D., Chapman, D. *et al.* (2006) 'Insights into Intimate Partner Violence from the Adverse Childhood Experiences (ACE) Study.' In P. Salber and E. Taliaferro (eds) *The Physician's Guide to Intimate Partner Violence and Abuse.* Volcano, CA: Volcano Press.

Anderson, K. (2001) 'Recovery: Resistance and resilience in female incest survivors.' *Dissertation Abstracts 62*, 09, 3185A.

Anderson, K. and Danis, F. (2007) 'Adult daughters of battered women: Resistance and resilience in the face of danger.' *Journal of Women and Social Work 21*, 4, 419–32.

Aris, R., Hague, G. and Mullender, A. (2003) 'Defined by Men's Abuse: The "Spoiled Identity" of Domestic Violence Survivors.' In B. Stanko (ed.) *The Meanings of Violence.* London: Routledge.

Bancroft, L. and Silverman, J. (2002) *The Batterer as Parent: Addressing the Impact of Domestic Violence on Family Dynamics.* Thousand Oaks, CA: Sage.

Banyard, V. and Williams, L. (2007) 'Women's voices on recovery: A multi-method study of the complexity of recovery from child sexual abuse.' *Child Abuse and Neglect 31*, 3, 274–90.

Banyard, V., Williams, L., Saunders, B. and Fitzgerald, M. (2008) 'The complexity of trauma types in the lives of women in families referred for family violence: Multiple mediators of mental health.' *American Journal of Orthopsychiatry 78*, 394–404.

Banyard, V., Williams, L. and Siegel, J. (2001) 'The long-term mental health consequences of child sexual abuse: An exploratory study of the impact of multiple traumas in a sample of women.' *Journal of Traumatic Stress 14*, 4, 97–715.

Becker-Blease, K. and Freyd, J. (2006) 'Research participants telling the truth about their lives: The ethics of asking and not asking about abuse.' *American Psychology 61*, 3, 218–26.

Bohn, D. and Holz, K. (1996) 'Health effects of childhood sexual abuse, domestic battering, and rape.' *Journal of Nurse-Midwifery 41*, 6, 442–56.

Boyer, D. and Fine, D. (1992) 'Sexual abuse as a factor in adolescent pregnancy and child maltreatment.' *Family Planning Perspectives 24*, 4–10.

Brandon, M. and Lewis, A. (1996) 'Significant harm and children's experiences of domestic violence.' *Child and Family Social Work 1*, 33–42.

Bridge Child Care Consultancy Service (1991) *Sukina: An Evaluation of the Circumstances Leading to her Death*. London: Bridge Child Care Consultancy Service.

Briere, J. and Jordan, C. (2009) 'Childhood maltreatment, intervening variables and adult psychological difficulties in women: An overview.' *Trauma, Violence and Abuse 10*, 375–84.

Briere, J. and Scott, C. (2007) 'Assessment of trauma symptoms in eating-disordered populations.' *Eating Disorders: The Journal of Treatment and Prevention 15*, 1–12.

Briere, J., Kaltman, S. and Green, B. (2008) 'Accumulated childhood trauma and symptom complexity.' *Journal of Traumatic Stress 21*, 223–26.

Cameron, C., Lau, C. and Tapanya, S. (2009) 'Passing it on during a 'day in the life' of resilient adolescents in diverse communities around the globe.' *Child and Youth Care Forum 38*, 5, 227–71.

Cannon, E., Bonomi, A., Anderson, M., Rivara, F. and Thompson, F. (2010) 'Relationship and health outcomes in women with a history of abuse and witnessing violence in childhood.' *Violence and Victims 25*, 3, 291–305.

Capaldi, D. and Clark, S. (1998) 'Prospective family predictors of aggression toward female partners for at-risk young men.' *Developmental Psychology 34*, 1175–88.

Cattanach, A. (1994) *Where the Sky Meets the Underworld*. London: Jessica Kingsley Publishers.

Cawson, P. (2002) *Child Maltreatment in the Family*. London: National Society for the Prevention of Cruelty to Children (NSPCC).

Cleaver, H., Walker, S., Scott, J., Cleaver, D. *et al.* (2007) *The Integrated Children's System Enhancing Social Work and Inter-Agency Practice*. London: Jessica Kingsley Publishers.

Clements, C., Oxtoby, C. and Ogle, R. (2008) 'Methodological issues in assessing psychological adjustment in children witnesses of intimate personal violence.' *Trauma, Violence and Abuse 9*, 2, 114–27.

Community Care (2011) *Council Cuts Leave Most Women's Refuges Facing Closure*. Available at www.communitycare.co.uk/Articles/08/03/2011/116416/council-cuts-leave-most-womens-refuges-facing-closure.htm, accessed 8 May 2011.

Copeland, M. and Harris, M. (2000) *Healing the Trauma of Abuse: A Women's Workbook*. Oakland, CA: New Harbinger Publications.

Copley, B. and Forryan, B. (1997) *Therapeutic Work with Children and Young People*. Cassell: London.

Department of Health (DoH) (2005) *Responding to Domestic Abuse: A Handbook for Health Professionals*. London: DoH.

Department of Health (DoH) and Home Office (2000) *No Secrets: Guidance on Developing and Implementing Multi-agency Policies and Procedures to Protect Vulnerable Adults from Abuse*. London: DoH.

Dietz, C. (2000) 'Responding to oppression and abuse: A feminist challenge to clinical social work.' *Affilia 15*, 369–89.

Dobash, R. and Dobash, R. (1992) *Women, Violence and Social Change.* London: Routledge.

Domestic Abuse, Stalking and Honour-based Violence (DASH) (2009) *Domestic Abuse, Stalking and Harassment and Honour-based Violence Risk Identification and Assessment and Management Model.* London: Association of Chief Police Officers (ACPO) and Co-ordinated Action Against Domestic Abuse (CAADA).

Donovan, C., Hester, M., McCarry, M. and Holmes, J. (2006) Comparing Domestic Abuse in Same Sex and Heterosexual Relationships. Bristol: Universities of Bristol and Sunderland.

Doob, S. (1992) 'Female sexual abuse survivors as patients: Avoiding retraumatization.' *Archives of Psychiatric Nursing 4,* 245–51.

Dube, S., Anda, R., Felitti, V., Chapman, D. *et al.* (2001) 'Childhood abuse, household dysfunction, and the risk of attempted suicide throughout the life span: Findings from the adverse childhood experiences study.' *Journal of the American Medical Association 286,* 3089–96.

Dube, S., Anda, R., Felitti, V., Edwards, V. and Williamson, D. (2002) 'Exposure to abuse, neglect and household dysfunction among adults who witnessed intimate partner violence as children: Implications for health and social services.' *Violence and Victims 17,* 1, 3–17.

Edleson, J. (1999) 'Children witnessing of adult domestic violence.' *Journal of Interpersonal Violence 14,* 839–70.

Edwards, V., Anda, R., Dube, S., Dong, M., Chapman, D. and Felitti, V. (2005) 'The Wide-Ranging Health Consequences of Adverse Childhood Experiences.' In K. Kendall-Tackett and S. Giacomoni (eds) *Victimization of Children and Youth: Patterns of Abuse, Response Strategies.* Kingston, NJ: Civic Research Institute.

Elbow, M. (1982) 'Children of violent marriages: The forgotten victims.' *Social Casework 63,* 465–71.

Ellis, J., Stanley, N. and Bell, J. (2006) 'Prevention Programmes for Children and Young People.' In C. Humphreys and N. Stanley (eds) *Domestic Violence and Child Protection: Directions for Good Practice.* London: Jessica Kingsley Publishers.

Ehrensaft, M., Cohen, P., Brown, J., Smailes, E., Chen, H. and Johnson, J. (2003) 'Intergenerational transmission of partner violence: A 20 year prospective study.' *Journal of Consulting and Clinical Psychology 71,* 4, 741–53.

Everett, B. and Gallop, R. (2001) *The Link between Childhood Trauma and Mental Illness: Effective Interventions for Mental Health Professions.* London: Sage.

Fantuzzo, J., Bruch, R., Beriama, A., Atkins, M. and Marcus, S. (1997) 'Domestic violence and children: Prevalence and risk in five major US cities.' *Journal of the American Academy of Child and Adolescent Psychiatry 36,* 1, 116–22.

Farmer, E. (2006) 'Using Research to Develop Child Protection and Child Care Practice.' In C. Humphreys and N. Stanley (eds) *Domestic Violence and Child Protection: Directions for Good Practice.* London: Jessica Kingsley Publishers.

Farmer, E. and Owen, M. (1995) *Child Protection Practice: Private Risks and Public Remedies.* London: HMSO.

Feerick, M. and Haugaard, J. (1999) 'Long-term effects of witnessing marital violence for women: The contribution of childhood physical and sexual abuse.' *Journal of Family Violence 14*, 4, 377–98.

Feldman, C. (1997) 'Childhood precursors of adult inter-partner violence.' *Clinical Psychology: Science and Practice 4*, 307–34.

Felitti, V., Anda, R., Nordenberg, D., Williamson, D. *et al.* (1998) 'Relationship of childhood abuse and household dysfunction to many of the leading causes of death in adults: The adverse childhood experiences (ACE) study.' *American Journal of Preventive Medicine 14*, 245–58.

Fife, R. and Shrager, S. (2011) *Family Violence: What Health Care Providers Need to Know.* Sudbury, MA: Jones and Bartlett Publishers.

Finkelhor, D. and Browne, A. (1986) 'Impact of child sexual abuse: A review of the research.' *Psychological Bulletin 99*, 66–77.

Folkman, S. and Lazarus, R. (1980) 'An analysis of coping in a middle-aged community sample.' *Journal of Health and Social Behavior 21*, 219–39.

Foucault, M. (1972) *The Archaeology of Knowledge* (A.M. Sheridan Smith, trans.). New York: Pantheon Books.

Freyd, J., Putnam, F., Lyon, T., Becker-Blease, K. *et al.* (2005) 'The science of child sexual abuse.' *Science 309*, 1183–4.

Gadd, D, Farrall, S., Lombard, N. and Dallimore, D. (2002) *Domestic Abuse Against Men in Scotland.* Edinburgh: Scottish Executive.

Gangoli, G., Razak, A. and McCarry, M. (2006) *Forced Marriage and Domestic Violence among South Asian Communities in North East England.* Bristol: University of Bristol.

Garmezy, N. (1983) 'Stressors of Childhood.' In N. Garmezy and M. Rutter (eds) *Stress, Coping, and Development in Children* (pp.43–84). New York: McGraw-Hill.

Garmezy, N. and Rutter, M. (1983) *Stress, Coping and Development in Children.* New York: McGraw-Hill.

Gill, A. (2006) 'Patriarchal violence in the name of "honour".' *International Journal of Criminal Justice Sciences 1*, 1, 1–12.

Gladstone, G., Parker, G., Mitchell, P., Malhi, G., Wilhelm, K. and Austin, M. (2004) 'Implications of childhood trauma for depressed women: An analysis of pathways from childhood sexual abuse to deliberate self-harm and revictimization.' *American Journal of Psychiatry 161*, 1417–25.

Glantz, M. and Johnson, J. (eds) (1999) *Resilience and Development: Positive Life Adaptations.* New York: Kluwer Academic Publishers.

Goodman, L. and Epstein, D. (2008) *Listening to Battered Women: A Survivor-centred Approach to Advocacy, Mental Health and Justice.* Washington, DC: American Psychological Association.

Goodman, L., Glenn, C., Bohlig, A., Banyard, V. and Borges, A. (2009) 'Feminist relational advocacy: Processes and outcomes from the perspective of low-income women with depression.' *The Counselling Psychologist 37*, 6, 848–76.

Grotberg, E. (1995) *A Guide to Promoting Resilience in Children, Strengthening the Human Spirit* (Early Childhood Development: Practice and Reflections series). The Netherlands: Bernard Van Leer Foundation.

Grotberg, E. (1997) 'The International Resilience Project.' In M. John (ed.) *A Charge Against Society: The Child's Right to Protection*. London: Jessica Kingsley Publishers.

Grych, J., Jouries, E., Swank, P., McDonald, R. and Norwood, W. (2000) 'Patterns of adjustment among children of battered women.' *Journal of Consulting and Clinical Psychology 68*, 84–94.

Hague, G. (2000) 'The silenced pain.' *Journal of Gender Studies 9*, 2, 157–65.

Hague, G. and Malos, E. (1993) *Domestic Violence: Action for Change*. Cheltenham: New Clarion Press.

Hague, G. and Malos, E. (2005, 3rd edn) *Domestic Violence: Action for Change*. Cheltenham: New Clarion Press.

Hague, G. and Sardinha, L. (2010) 'Violence against women: Devastating legacy and transforming services.' *Psychiatry, Psychology and Law 17*, 4, 503–22.

Hague, G. and Wilson, C. (1996) *The Silenced Pain: Domestic Violence 1945–1970*. Bristol: The Policy Press.

Hague, G., Kelly, L. and Mullender, A. (2001) *Challenging Violence against Women: The Canadian Experience*. Bristol: The Policy Press.

Hague, G., Malos, E. and Dear, W. (1996) *Multi-agency Work and Domestic Violence*. Bristol: The Policy Press.

Hague, G., Mullender, A. and Aris, R. (2003) *Is Anyone Listening? Accountability and Women Survivors of Domestic Violence*. London: Routledge.

Hague, G., Mullender, A., Kelly, L., Malos, E. and Debbonaire, T. (2000) 'Unsung Innovation: The History of Work with Children in UK Domestic Violence Refuges.' In J. Hanmer, C. Itzen, S. Quaid and D. Wigglesworth (eds) *Home Truths about Domestic Violence. Feminist Influences on Policy and Practice: A Reader*. London: Routledge.

Hague, G., Thiara, R., Mullender, A. and Magowan, P. (2008) *Making the Links: Disabled Women and Domestic Violence*. Good Practice Guide and Full Report, both available from Bristol: Women's Aid Federation of England. Available at www.womensaid. org.uk/core/core_picker/download.asp?id=1763, accessed 3 January 2011, and at www.bristol.ac.uk/vawrg, www.warwick.ac.uk.

Harding, S. (1987) *Feminism and Methodology: Social Science Issues*. Bloomington: Indiana University Press.

Harvey, M. (1996) 'An ecological view of psychological trauma and trauma recovery.' *Journal of Traumatic Stress 9*, 3–23.

Hayes, E. and Flannery, D. (2000) *Women as Learners: The Significance of Gender in Adult Learning*. San Francisco, CA: Jossey-Bass Inc. Publishers.

Hendricks, J., Kaplan, T. and Black, D. (1993) *When Father Kills Mother: Guiding Children through Trauma and Grief*. London: Routledge.

Henning, K., Leitenberg, H., Coffey, P., Turner, T. and Bennett, R. (1996) 'Long-term psychological consequences in women of witnessing parental physical conflict and experiencing abuse in childhood.' *Journal of Interpersonal Violence 11*, 5–51.

Herman, J. (1992) 'Complex PTSD: A syndrome of prolonged and repeated trauma.' *Journal of Traumatic Stress 5*, 3, 377–91.

Herman, J. (1997, 3rd edn) *Trauma and Recovery: The Aftermath of Violence from Domestic Abuse to Political Terror*. New York: Basic Books.

Herman, J., Russell, D. and Trochi, K. (1986) 'Long-term effects of incestuous abuse in childhood. *American Journal of Psychiatry 143*, 1293–6.

Hester, M. (2009) *Who Does What to Whom? Gender and Domestic Violence Perpetrators*. Bristol: University of Bristol in association with the Northern Rock Foundation.

Hester, M. (2011) 'The three-planet model: Towards an understanding of contradictions in approaches to women and children's safety in contexts of domestic violence.' *British Journal of Social Work 41*, 837–53.

Hester, M. and Pearson, C. (1998) *From Periphery to Centre: Domestic Violence in Work with Abused Children*. Bristol: The Policy Press.

Hester, M. and Radford, L. (1996) *Domestic Violence and Child Contact Arrangements in England and Denmark*. Bristol: The Policy Press.

Hester, M., Pearson, C. and Harwin, N. with Abrahams, H. (2007, 2nd edn) *Making an Impact: Children and Domestic Violence*. London: Jessica Kingsley Publishers.

Hideout, The (2011) *The Hideout: Until Children and Young People are Safe*. Available at www.thehideout.org.uk, accessed on 21 August 2011.

Hilberg, T. (2011) 'Review of meta-analyses on the association between child sexual abuse and adult mental health difficulties: A systematic approach.' *Trauma Violence and Abuse 1*, 12, 38–49.

Hobfoll, S. (2002) 'Social and psychological resources and adaptations.' *Review of General Psychology 6*, 302–24.

Home Office (2011) *Call to End Violence against Women and Girls*. Available at www.homeoffice.gov.uk/crime/violence-against-women-girls/strategic-vision, accessed 5 April 2011.

Houghton, C. (2006) 'Listen Louder: Working with children and young people.' In C. Humphreys and N. Stanley (eds) *Domestic Violence and Child Protection*. London: Jessica Kingsley Publishers.

Howe, D. (2005) *Child Abuse and Neglect: Attachment, Development and Intervention*. London: Palgrave Macmillan.

Howes, R. (2010) 'The ten coolest therapy interventions.' *Psychology Today*. Available at www.psychologytoday.com/blog/in-therapy/201001/the-ten-coolest-therapy-interventions-introduction, accessed 17 January 2010.

Hughes, H., Graham-Bermann, S. and Gruber, G. (2001) 'Resilience in Children Exposed to Domestic Violence.' In J. Edleson (ed.) *Domestic Violence in the Lives of Children: The Future of Research, Intervention and Social Policy*. Washington, DC: American Psychological Association.

Humphreys, C. (2006) 'Thinking the Unthinkable: The Implications of Research on Women and Children in Relation to Domestic Violence.' In Rt Hon. Lord Justice Thorpe and R. Budden (eds) *Durable Solutions: Collected Papers of the 2005 Dartington Hall Conference*. Bristol: Jordan Publishing.

Humphreys, C. and Stanley, N. (ed.) (2006) *Domestic Violence and Child Protection: Directions for Good Practice*. London: Jessica Kingsley Publishers.

Humphreys, C. and Thiara, R. (2002) *Routes to Safety: Protection Issues Facing Abused Women and Children and the Role of Outreach Services.* Bristol: Women's Aid.

Humphreys, C., Hague, G., Hester, M. and Mullender, A. (2000) *From Good Intentions to Good Practice.* Warwick: Centre for the Study of Well-being, University of Warwick

Humphreys, C., Thiara, R. and Skamballis, A. (2010) 'Readiness for change: Mother–child relationships and domestic violence intervention.' *British Journal of Social Work 40*, 166–84.

Humphreys, C., Thiara, R., Skamballis, A. and Mullender, A. (2006) *Talking to My Mum: A Picture Workbook for Workers, Mothers and Children Affected by Domestic Abuse.* London: Jessica Kingsley Publishers.

Humphreys, J. (2001) 'Turnings and adaptations in resilient daughters of battered women.' *Journal of Nursing Scholarship 33*, 245–51.

Imam, U. and Akhtar, P. (2005) 'Researching Asian Children's Experiences of Domestic Violence: The Significance of Cultural Competence and Shared Ethnicities of Participants in the Research Process.' In T. Skinner, M. Hester and E. Malos (eds) *Researching Gender Violence: Feminist Methodology in Action.* Devon: Willan Publishing.

Iwaniec, D. (2006, 2nd edn) *The Emotionally Abused and Neglected Child: Identification, Assessment and Intervention. A Practice Handbook.* Chichester: John Wiley and Sons.

Iwaniec, D., Larkin, E. and Higgins, S. (2006) 'Research review: Risk and resilience in cases of emotional abuse.' *Child and Family Social Work 11*, 73–82.

Jaffe, P., Baker, L. and Cunningham, A. (eds) (2004) *Protecting Children from Domestic Violence.* London: Guilford Press.

Jaffe, P., Wolfe, D. and Wilson, S. (1990) *Children of Battered Women.* Newbury Park, CA: Sage Publications.

James, B. (1996) *Treating Traumatized Children: New Insights and Creative Interventions.* New York: Free Press.

James, M. (1994) 'Domestic violence a form of child abuse identification and prevention.' *Issues in Child Abuse and Prevention 2*, 1–14.

Kaplow, J., Dodge, K., Amaya-Jackson, L. and Saxe, G. (2005) 'Pathways to PTSD, Part II: Sexually abused children.' *American Journal of Psychiatry 162*, 1305–10.

Kashani, J. and Allan, W. (1998) *The Impact of Family Violence on Children and Adolescents.* Thousand Oaks, CA: Sage Publications.

Kelly, L. (1988) *Surviving Sexual Violence.* Cambridge: Polity Press.

Kelly, L. (1994) 'The Interconnectedness of Domestic Violence and Child Abuse.' In A. Mullender and R. Morley (eds) *Children Living with Domestic Violence.* London: Whiting and Birch.

Kelly, L. and Radford, J. (1998) 'Sexual Violence Against Women and Girls: An Approach to an International Overview.' In R. Dobash and R. Dobash (eds) *Rethinking Violence Against Women.* Thousand Oaks, CA: Sage.

Kendall-Tackett, K. and Becker-Blease, K. (2004) 'The importance of retrospective findings in child maltreatment research.' *Child Abuse and Neglect 28*, 7, 723–27.

Kerley, K., Xu, X., Sirisunyaluck, B. and Alley, J. (2010) 'Exposure to family violence in childhood and intimate partner perpetration or victimization in adulthood: Exploring intergenerational transmission in urban Thailand.' *Journal of Family Violence 25*, 3, 337–47.

Kilpatrick, K., Litt, M. and Williams, L. (1997) 'Post-traumatic stress disorder in child witness to domestic violence.' *American Journal of Orthopsychiatry 67*, 4, 639–44.

Kitzmann, K., Gayford, N., Holt, A. and Kenny, E. (2003) 'Child witnesses to domestic violence: A meta-analytic review.' *Journal of Consulting and Clinical Psychology 71*, 2, 339–52.

Koss, M. and Burkhart, B. (1989) 'A conceptual analysis of rape victimization: Long-term effects and implications for treatment.' *Psychology of Women Quarterly 13*, 27–40.

Krinsley, K., Gallagher, J., Weathers, F., Kutter, C. and Kaloupek, D. (2003) 'Consistency of retrospective reporting about exposure to traumatic events.' *Journal of Traumatic Stress 16*, 399–409.

Kulkarni, M., Graham-Bermann, S., Rauch, S. and Seng, J. (2011) 'Witnessing versus experiencing direct violence in childhood as correlates of adulthood PTSD.' *Journal of Interpersonal Violence 26*, 6, 1264–81.

Kwong, M., Bartholomew, K., Henderson, A. and Trinke, S. (2003) 'The intergenerational transmission of relationship violence.' *Journal of Family Psychology 17*, 288–301.

Lang, A., Stein, M., Kennedy, C. and Foy, D. (2004) 'Adult psychopathology and intimate partner violence among survivors of childhood maltreatment.' *Journal of Interpersonal Violence 19*, 10, 1102–18.

Leeners, B., Stiller, R., Block, E., Gorres, G., *et al.* (2007) 'Consequences of childhood sexual abuse experiences on dental care.' *Journal of Psychosomatic Research 62*, 5, 581–88.

Levondosky, A., Bogat, G. and von Eye, A. (2000) *Risk and Protective Factors for Domestic Violence*. Atlanta, GA: Centers for Disease Control, Injury Prevention Center.

Lowe, P., Humphreys, C. and Williams, S. (2008) 'Night terrors: Women's experiences of (not) sleeping where there is domestic violence.' *Violence against Women 13*, 6, 549–61.

Luthar, S., Cicchetti, D. and Becker, B. (2000) 'The construct of resilience: A critical evaluation and guideline for future work.' *Child Development 7*, 543–62.

Margolin, G. and Gordis, E. (2000) 'The effect of family and community violence on children.' *Annual Review of Psychology 51*, 445–79.

Masten, A. (2001) 'Ordinary magic: Resilience processes in development.' *American Psychologist 56*, 227–38.

McCloskey, A. and Walker, M. (2000) 'Post-traumatic stress in children exposed to family violence and single-event trauma. *Journal of the American Academy of Child and Adolescent Psychiatry 39*, 1, 108–15.

McGee, C. (2000) *Childhood Experiences of Domestic Violence*. London: Jessica Kingsley Publishers.

McQueen, D., Itzin, C., Kennedy, R., Sinason, V. and Maxted, F. (2008) *Psychoanalytic Psychotherapy After Child Abuse: The Treatment of Adults and Children Who Have Experienced Sexual Abuse, Violence, and Neglect in Childhood.* London: Karnac Books Ltd.

Merrick, D. (2006, 2nd edn) *Social Work and Child Abuse: Still Walking the Tightrope.* London: Routledge.

Mertin, P. and Mohr, P. (2002) 'Incidence and correlates of posttrauma symptoms in children from background s of domestic violence.' *Violence and Victims 17*, 555–67.

Miller-Perrin, C. and Perrin, R. (2007) *Child Maltreatment: An Introduction.* Thousand Oaks, CA: Sage Publications.

Moon, M. (2000) 'Retrospective reports of interparental abuse by adult children from intact families'. *Journal of Interpersonal Violence*, 15, 1323–1331.

Mouzos, J. and Makkai, T. (2004) *Women's Experiences of Male Violence: Findings from the Australian Component of the International Violence Against Women Survey (IVAWS).* Canberra: Australian Institute of Criminology.

Mullender, A. and Morley, R. (eds) (1994) *Children Living with Domestic Violence: Putting Men's Abuse of Women on the Childcare Agenda.* London: Whiting and Birch.

Mullender, A., Burton, S., Hague, G., Imam, U. *et al.* (2003) *Stop Hitting Mum!: Children Talk About Domestic Violence.* East Molesey, Surrey: Young Voice.

Mullender, A., Hague, I., Imam, U., Kelly, L., Malos, E. and Regan, L. (2002) *Children's Perspectives on Domestic Violence.* London: Sage Publications.

Oaklander, V. (1978) *Windows to Our Children: A Gestalt Therapy Approach to Children and Adolescents.* Boulder, CO: Real People Press.

O'Hara, M. (1994) 'Child Deaths in the Context of Domestic Violence.' In A. Mullender and R. Morley (eds) *Children Living with Domestic Violence.* London: Whiting and Birch.

Peled, E. (1993) *The Experience of Living with Violence for Preadolescent Witnesses of Woman Abuse.* Unpublished doctoral dissertation. Minneapolis, MN: University of Minnesota.

Peled, E. (1997) 'Intervention with children of battered women: A review of the current literature.' *Children and Youth Services Review 19*, 4, 277–99.

Peled, E. and Davis, D. (1995) *Groupwork with Children of Battered Women.* Thousand Oaks, CA: Sage.

Peled, E. and Edleson, J. (1992) 'Multiple perspectives on groupwork with children of battered women.' *Violence and Victims 7*, 327–46.

Radford, L. and Hester, M. (2006) *Mothering Through Domestic Violence.* London: Jessica Kingsley Publishers.

Radford, L., Corral, S., Bradley, C., Fisher, H. *et al.* (2011) *Child Abuse and Neglect in the UK Today.* London: National Society for the Prevention of Cruelty to Children (NSPCC).

Rights of the Child UK (ROCK) (2011) *For the Incorporation of the United Nations Convention on the Rights of the Child into UK Law 2010.* London: Children's Rights Alliance for England.

Rivett, M. and Kelly, S. (2006) 'From awareness to practice: Children, domestic violence and child welfare.' *Child Abuse Review 15*, 224–42.

Rivett, M., Howarth, E. and Harold, G. (2006) 'Practice in work with child witnesses of domestic violence.' *Clinical Child Psychology and Psychiatry 11*, 1, 103–25.

Rosenbaum, A. and O'Leary, D. (1981) 'Children: The unintended victims of marital violence.' *American Journal of Orthopsychiatry 51*, 692–99.

Rossman, B. (1998) 'Descartes' Error and Posttraumatic Stress Disorder: Cognition and Emotion in Children who are Exposed to Parental Violence.' In G.W. Holden, R. Geffner and E.N. Jouriles (eds) *Children Exposed to Marital Violence*. Washington, DC: American Psychological Association.

Rutter, M. (1985) 'Resilience in the face of adversity: Protective factors and resistance to psychiatric disorder.' *British Journal of Psychiatry 147*, 598–611.

Sanderson, C. (2008) *Counselling Survivors of Domestic Abuse*. London: Jessica Kingsley Publishers.

Saunders, H. (2004) *Twenty-nine Child Homicides: Lessons Still to be Learnt on Domestic Violence and Child Protection*. Bristol: Women's Aid.

Saunders, H. and Barron, J. (2003) *Failure to Protect? Domestic Violence and the Experiences of Abused Women and Children in the Family Courts*. Bristol: Women's Aid.

Scottish Women's Aid (2011) *Listen Louder*. Available at www.scottishwomensaid.org.uk/influencing-and-campaigning/previous-campaigns/listen-louder, accessed 8 August 2011.

Silvern, L., Karyl, J., Waelde, L., Hodges, W. *et al.* (1995) 'Retrospective reports of parental partner abuse: Relationships to depression, trauma symptoms and self-esteem among college students.' *Journal of Family Violence 10*, 2, 177–202.

Skogrand, L., DeFrain, J., DeFrain, N. and Jones, J. (2007) *Surviving and Transcending a Traumatic Childhood: The Dark Thread* (Haworth Series in Marriage and Family Studies). London: Routledge.

Sousa, C., Herrenkohl, T., Moylan, C., Tajima, E. *et al.* (2011) 'Longitudinal study on the effects of child abuse and children's exposure to domestic violence, parent–child attachments, and antisocial behaviour in adolescence.' *Journal of Interpersonal Violence 26*, 1, 111–36.

Stanley, N. (2011) *Children Experiencing Domestic Violence: A Research Review*. Dartington: Research into Practice.

Stanley, N., Miller, P., Richardson Foster, H. and Thomson, G. (2010) 'A stop–start response: Social services, interventions with children and families notified following domestic violence incidents.' *British Journal of Social Work 40*, 1–18.

Stark, E. (2007) *Coercive Control: The Entrapment of Women in Personal Life*. Oxford: Oxford University Press.

Stith, S., Rosen, M., Middleton, K., Busch, A., Lundeberg, K. and Carlton, R. (2000) 'The intergenerational transmission of spouse abuse: A meta-analysis.' *Journal of Marriage and the Family 62*, 640–54.

Stone, H. and Stone, S. (1993a) *Embracing Our Selves: The Voice Dialogue Manual*. Navato, CA: Nataraj Publishing.

Stone, H. and Stone, S. (1993b) *Embracing Your Inner Critic: Turning Self-criticism into a Creative Asset.* San Francisco, CA: Harper.

Straus, M. (1992) *Children as Witnesses to Marital Violence: A Risk Factor for Lifelong Problems among a Nationally Representative Sample of American Men and Women. Report of the Twenty-Third Ross Roundtable.* Columbus, OH: Ross Laboratories.

Straus, M. and Smith, C. (1990) 'Family Patterns and Child Abuse.' In M. Straus and R. Gelles (eds) *Physical Violence in American Families: Risk Factor Adaptations to Violence in 8,145 Families.* New Bruswick, NJ: Transaction Publishers.

Sturge, C. and Glaser, D. (2000) 'Contact and domestic violence: The Expert Court report.' *Family Law* September, 615–28.

Sugarman, D. and Frankel, S. (1996) 'Patriarchal ideology and wife assault: A meta-analytic review.' *Journal of Family Violence 11*, 13–40.

Sullivan, M., Egan, M. and Gooch, M. (2004) 'Conjoint interventions for adult victims and children of domestic violence: A program evaluation.' *Research on Social Work Practice 14*, 163–70.

Teicher, M., Samson, J., Polcari, A. and McGreenery, C. (2006) 'Sticks, stones, and hurtful words: Relative effects of various forms of childhood maltreatment.' *American Journal of Psychiatry 163*, 6, 993–1000.

Terr, L. (1994) *Unchained Memories: True Stories of Traumatic Memories, Lost and Found.* New York: HarperCollins Publishers.

Thiara, R. and Ellis, J. (2005) *WDVF London-wide School's Domestic Violence Prevention Project: An Evaluation.* London: Westminster Domestic Violence Forum.

Thiara, R. and Ellis, J. (forthcoming) *Working with Children and Young People to Address Violence Against Women and Girls: Lessons for Policy and Practice.* Bristol: The Policy Press.

Thiara, R. and Gill, A. (2011) *Domestic Violence, Child Contact and Post-Separation Violence: Issues for South Asian and African-Caribbean Women and Children.* London: National Society for the Prevention of Cruelty to Children (NSPCC).

Ungar, M. (2011) *Counseling in Challenging Contexts: Working with Individuals and Families across Clinical and Community Settings.* Belmont, CA: Brooks/Cole.

United Nations Assembly (1989) *UN Convention on the Rights of the Child.* New York: United Nations.

van der Kolk, B., MacFarlane, A. and Weisaeth, L. (2007) *Traumatic Stress: The Effects of Overwhelming Experience on Mind, Body, and Society.* Guilford: The Guilford Press.

Wade, A. (1997) 'Small acts of living: Everyday resistance to violence and other forms of oppression.' *Contemporary Family Therapy 19*, 23–39.

Walker, E., Newman, E., Koss, M. and Bernstein, D. (1997) 'Does the study of victimization revictimize the victims?' *Psychiatry and Primary Care 19*, 403–10.

Wekerle, C., Miller, A., Wolfe, D. and Spindel, C. (2006) *Childhood Maltreatment.* Cambridge, MA: Hogrefe and Huber.

Welchman, L. and Hossain, S. (eds) (2005) *'Honour': Crimes, Paradigms and Violence against Women,* London: Zed Press.

Whitfield, C., Anda, R., Dube, S. and Felitti, V. (2003) 'Violent childhood experiences and the risk of intimate partner violence in adults.' *Journal of Interpersonal Violence 18*, 166–85.

Widom, C. and Morris, S. (1997) 'Accuracy of adult recollections of childhood victimization. Part II: Childhood sexual abuse.' *Psychological Assessment 9*, 34–6.

Williams, L. (1994) 'Recall of childhood trauma: A prospective study of women's memories of child sexual abuse.' *Journal of Consulting and Clinical Psychology 62*, 1167–76.

Wilson, S., Cameron, S., Jaffe, P. and Wolfe, D. (1986) *Manual for a Group Program for Children Exposed to Wife Abuse.* London, Ontario: London Family Courts Clinic.

Wolfe, D., Crooks, D., Lee, V., McIntyre-Smith, A. and Jaffe, P. (2003) 'The effects of children's exposure to domestic violence: A meta-analysis and critique.' *Clinical Child and Family Psychology Review 6*, 3, 171–87.

Women's Aid (2007) What is domestic violence? Available at www.womensaid.org.uk/domestic-violence-articles.asp?section=00010001002200410001&itemid=1272. Accessed 21 January 2012.

Women's Aid (2011a) *Women Aid Survey Reveals Fear that Over Half of Refuge and Outreach Services could Face Closure.* Available at www.womensaid.org.uk/domestic-violence-press-information.asp?itemid=2599itemTitle=Women92s+surevy+reveals+fear+that+over+half+of+refuge+and+outreach+services+could+face+closure&section=00010001001050001&sectionTitle=Press+releases.

Women's Aid (2011b) *Survivor's Forum.* Available at www.womensaid.org.uk/Survivors-Forum, accessed 24 June 2011.

World Health Organisation (WHO) (2005) *WHO Multi-country Study on Women's Health and Domestic Violence against Women.* Geneva: WHO.

Worrall, A., Boylan, J. and Roberts, D. (2008) *SCIE Research Briefing 25: Children's and Young People's Experiences of Domestic Violence Involving Adults in a Parenting Role.* Available at www.scie.org.uk/publications/briefings/briefing25/index.asp, accessed 4 August 2011.

Subject Index

Author Index